UP FOR GRABS

A Florida Sand Dollar Book

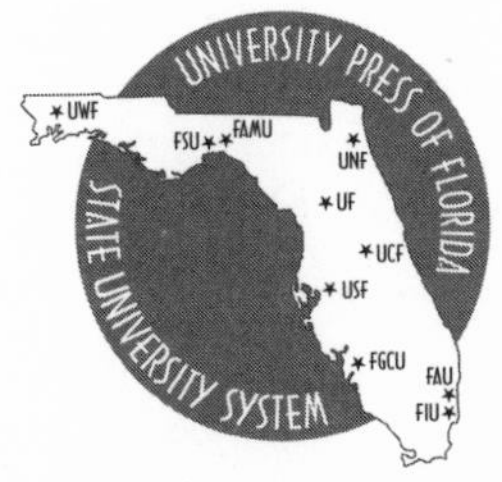

Florida A&M University, Tallahassee
Florida Atlantic University, Boca Raton
Florida Gulf Coast University, Ft. Myers
Florida International University, Miami
Florida State University, Tallahassee
University of Central Florida, Orlando
University of Florida, Gainesville
University of North Florida, Jacksonville
University of South Florida, Tampa
University of West Florida, Pensacola

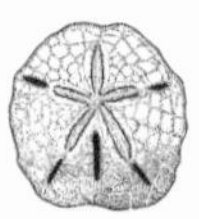

Florida Sand Dollar Books

Nine Florida Stories by Marjory Stoneman Douglas, edited by Kevin M. McCarthy (1990)
Flagler: Rockefeller Partner and Florida Baron, by Edward N. Akin (1992)
St. Petersburg and the Florida Dream, 1888–1950, by Raymond Arsenault (1996)
Southwest Florida's Wetland Wilderness: Big Cypress Swamp and the Ten Thousand Islands, by Jeff Ripple (1996)
The Immigrant World of Ybor City: Italians and Their Latin Neighbors in Tampa, 1885–1985, by Gary R. Mormino and George E. Pozzetta (1998)
Some Kind of Paradise, by Mark Derr (1998)
Surrounded on Three Sides, by John Keasler (1999)
Palmetto Leaves, by Harriet Beecher Stowe (1999)
Sunshine States: Wild Times and Extraordinary Lives in the Land of Gators, Guns and Grapefruit, by Patrick Carr (1999)
Contemplations of a Primal Mind, by Gabriel Horn (2000)
River of the Golden Ibis, by Gloria Jahoda (2000)
Going to Miami: Exiles, Tourists and Refugees in the New America, by David Rieff (2000)
Up for Grabs: A Trip Through Time and Space in the Sunshine State, by John Rothchild (2000)

UP FOR GRABS

A Trip Through Time and Space in the Sunshine State

John Rothchild

University Press of Florida
Gainesville Tallahassee Tampa Boca Raton
Pensacola Orlando Miami Jacksonville Ft. Myers

First printed in 1985 by Viking Penguin, Inc.
Printed in the United States of America on acid-free paper

05 04 03 02 01 00 6 5 4 3 2 1

Library of Congress cataloging-in-publication data are available.

The University Press of Florida is the scholarly publishing agency for the State University System of Florida, comprising Florida A&M University, Florida Atlantic University, Florida Gulf Coast University, Florida International University, Florida State University, University of Central Florida, University of Florida, University of North Florida, University of South Florida, and University of West Florida.

University Press of Florida
15 Northwest 15th Street
Gainesville, FL 32611–2079
http://www.upf.com

To Susan

A Muse with a Mind of Her Own

Acknowledgments

Joette Lorion, a single-handed research department; Amanda Vaill, a conscientious editor and ingenious collaborator; Phil Stanford; Bob and Polly Knox; Doug Balz; Jack Levy; Fred Dorsett; Marcia Rankin; Liz Darhansoff; Taylor Branch; Allen Morris, editor of Florida handbooks; the staff of the Florida collection at the University of Florida library; Frank Tenney; Florence Thomasson; Eileen Bernard; the Southwest Florida Regional Planning Council and especially Wayne Daltrey; Roland Eastwood; Harry Dietrich; Hilda Inclan; Liz Balmaseda; Carl Hiaasen; Ruth Cook; Morris, Bobby, and A. J. Wolf; Beth Dunlop; Stacy Schiff; the *Miami Herald* and the *Miami News* libraries, and especially Joe Wright; Irv Samuels; Al Burt; Vince Conboy; Jo and Diane Durden-Smith; Marjory Stoneman Douglas; Ed DeYoung; Margie Walker; Madeline Blais; and John Katzenbach.

For material about the mob in Florida, Hank Messick's book, *Lansky*, G. P. Putnam's Sons, New York, 1971; for material about the pirate Gaspar, Karl Bickel's book, *The Mangrove Coast*, Coward-McCann, Inc., New York, 1961; for material about Al Capone, Gene Burnett's article in the September 1978 edition of *Florida Trend* magazine.

A special thanks to Mitchell Kaplan, owner of Miami's most inviting bookstore and the force behind Miami's celebrated annual book fair, who spent considerable time and effort to give this narrative a second life. Thanks to the University Press of Florida staff, particularly Meredith Babb and Deidre Bryan, for launching the new edition. Thanks to John Dorshner of the *Miami Herald*, Mike Clary of the *Los Angeles Times*, and Tom Austin of *Ocean Drive* magazine for help with updating and fact checking. Cathy Leff at Miami Beach's Wolfsonian Museum has dutifully passed around dog-eared copies, and I'm grateful to many other friends who've kept the book on their bookshelves. I've snooped around and noticed who has and who hasn't.

Contents

UP FOR GRABS

Reentry

Miami, August 1972. From the airport, it is a cab ride across Biscayne Bay to Miami Beach, site of the Republican National Convention. The cab passes a golf course, where the sprinkler system is working nights. The atmosphere is that of a sauna. The sun has been down for two hours, but there is still pink in the horizon. Airplanes in the landing pattern search the thunderheads with their beams. The illumination of the clouds makes them cherubic; the clouds and the pink horizon, visible in the general obscurity, suggest a Tiepolo, as viewed through sunglasses.

An assignment to cover the Republicans brought me from Washington, D.C., my adopted residence, back to Florida, where I was raised. Being raised Floridian means that I moved here from Connecticut when I was seven years old, with parents who came out of the Midwest, transferred to the Northeast, retreated to Florida, and then left as soon as it was convenient, as soon as the children were grown.

The state's population nearly doubled in the 1950s and doubled again from 1960 to 1980, making it probable that one's Florida neighbors had originated elsewhere. Of course, all states are composed of people from elsewhere, but Florida in the years of my childhood was the extreme of elsewhereness, with a majority of residents having just arrived in the present decade. The difference between tourist and resident was only a matter of a season's inhabitance, last season's tourist was this season's Floridian.

What great distinctions we made over short time spans, perhaps based on our own insecurities about our claim to this place. It is analogous, I think, to the insecurity over racial purity that produced all the distinctions of color (octoroon and so forth) in the French colonies. In Florida, a five-year resident was taken for a native, and could then pose as an expert on mildew and heat prostration to the tourist. A ten-year resident was a hoary ancestor, who probably remembered a hurricane. A twenty-year resident was a remarkable creature, an oddity really.

On the east and west coasts where most of the newcomers live, a child who grew up in Florida was given the kind of deference that in New England is reserved for those few Daughters of the American Revolution. Here we achieved it without having to wait any two centuries, and so while I entered the schools as a newcomer in third grade, by the time of the tenth I was counted among the old-timers. Native Floridians, that is, those few people who go back more than one generation, were so exceptional that they lost status, their tenure so unbelievable that it was irrelevant to the rest of us. I am a nominal Floridian, but the nominal Floridian is the typical Floridian, as opposed to the native Floridian, who is unusual and feels like a stranger.

We made the trip from Connecticut to Florida in the summer of 1953. The car seat smelled of breakfast jelly. The blob that must have dropped from a piece of toast was now only a stain on the gray upholstery; the heat revived its odor. We drove through the center of every eastern seaboard city from New York to Savannah. There were no bypasses. The cat was shedding in a wicker basket, the air from the open car windows brought flurries of dander across our faces. The dog panted as if it had rabies. It tried to run away at gas stations.

Like Icarus we fled to sunshine, two children, two pets, loosed from the New England suburbs, stuck in our own sweat to those seats redolent of jelly, forced to refresh ourselves at segregated drinking fountains, emerging from cheap motels to be transported closer and closer to the primary solar source.

My father saw everything as a learning opportunity. Our stifling confinement was his mobile classroom; he expected us to absorb history and culture through the windshield. For three hours in the midday summer traffic jam, we absorbed the marble steps of Baltimore. That great Florida invention, the air conditioner, originally intended to soothe victims of malaria, was not yet attached to cars that we could afford.

To avert mutiny from his captive audience, my father announced that we would stop at a motel and then get up and drive at night, when it would be cooler. It would also be too dark to learn. Already we compromised with the latitude: northern industry sacrificed to southern comfort, and we hadn't even reached the Florida border.

My sister and I prepared for a volatile increase in temperature that never occurred. Florida was no hotter than Georgia. We drove by day during part of that last 200 miles, the north Florida landscape seemed anemic and somehow depressing, like the pencil sketches on the covers of ragtime piano sheet music. My spirits were improved by the Florida gift shops, which doubled as orange juice counters and gas stations. My father preferred to pay for his gas and leave. "These are tourist traps," he grumbled.

For a child's affection, there was no contest between the

drab road and the brilliant tourist traps, with their bags of Day-Glo citrus bunkered around the legs of giant billboards twice the size of the adjacent buildings, billboards whose own colors were the equal of the most luminous highway caution cone or police rain slicker. It was at such a tourist trap that I got my first glimpse of the Rebel flag terry-cloth beach towel, Florida's special contribution to Civil War tourist trap memorabilia. In Georgia and the Carolinas, the Dixie grudge was expressed on bumpers and windshields, but here you could lie down on it, a prospect that both astounded and reassured a Yankee browser. If you could lie down on Dixie in Florida, perhaps you could lie down on anything.

A hedonistic surrealism replaced all the roadside historic themes from the gas stations of the other eastern states. Black mammy syrup jars and butter dishes shaped like plantations were absent from Florida's shelves, which instead were taken up with coconut heads carved to look like pirates, pelicans made from seashells, tiny crates of bubble-gum oranges, fish skulls advertised as souvenirs of the Crucifixion, seahorses dried and packaged like aquatic beef jerky, perfume tapped from tangerines, stuffed alligators, cans of sunshine, and postcards of beauty queens in low-cut bathing suits, stooped in the groves like migrant fruit pickers, with their half-exposed breasts competing favorably with the fruit.

Whatever culture these things represented—and that the seven-year-old found irresistible—was not what brought my family to Florida. We sought the physical and the economic cure. I had asthma, and the hope that Florida might bake out my illness was the hope that populated St. Petersburg, our destination, with invalids sixty years my senior. My father had money worries; the schoolteacher's salary in Connecticut was insufficient to cover expenses.

Prior to having become a teacher, my father studied Russian at Columbia University while working part-time as an elevator operator at the New York Stock Exchange. Any man who read Bolshevik literature, even as he lifted capitalists to their daily transactions, would not have been hired in some U.S. school districts in the McCarthy years. But by the time we came to Florida, McCarthyism had waned. The state was growing fast, and county school systems along its west coast were desperate for qualified teachers.

The salary was low, lower than in Connecticut, but a Florida teacher could live better on less. The sunshine was an extra employee benefit, potentially more valuable than medical insurance; for me, it was free asthma treatment. And in Florida, there was a constitutional amendment against an income tax, as if an income tax were an affront to basic human rights.

These were the Florida advantages for which my father, a Russian scholar, a sentimental populist, a registered Democrat, and an extremely industrious man, elected to become a resident of a Gulf of Mexico resort, dominated by old Republicans in the exile of retirement and playing golf as their last reward, the golf course serving as the very landscape of afterlife.

In 1972, I was twenty-seven years old and disinterested in Florida per se. I was not interested in Republicans either, but a friend who had been to the earlier Democratic convention, also held on Miami Beach, returned with some intriguing stories about a mansion on North Bay Road, owned by a generous and eccentric heiress, who offered free room and board to anybody who opposed Nixon. The friend had said there was plenty of "acid" at this mansion, and I had heard only the first syllable. I was getting a divorce. Selective perception led me to seek the assignment to cover the Republicans, the assignment that resulted in my Florida reentry.

The airport cab took me along North Bay Road, where Spanish-style houses were hidden behind stucco walls and subtropical foliage, and between the houses and their outbuildings and the landscaping was an occasional glimpse of nocturnal reflections off Biscayne Bay. At the front entrance I was met by a small, bearded greeter who wore a beaded skullcap. With the cap and white beard, he looked enchanted.

Behind the greeter, men in gauze pants and women in leotards were taking communion from a platter of synthetic mescaline. Behind them, other people lolled in the pool. At the edge of the pool a film of the wedding of President Nixon's eldest daughter, Tricia—as reenacted by a group of transvestites called the Cockettes—was shown against a white stucco wall and leeched out into the clouds. The dining room table was loaded with delicatessen food. The proximity of the deli bar to the drugs produced a Miami Beach cultural adaptation: the mescaline bagel.

The mansion was the informal headquarters for the hippie-yippie coalition and the anti-Nixon left. The inhabitants agonized at poolside about the bombing of Cambodia; they advocated the end of militarism between snorts; they decried Nixon's fascism while improving their suntans. There was a nightly antiwar demonstration outside the convention headquarters or down at Flamingo Park, where other protestors camped out and agonized over the bombing of Cambodia, but in less favorable circumstances.

The convention organizers talked of raising the bridges to the mainland, if necessary, to contain the dissent on this side of Biscayne Bay. Nobody realized, at the time, that Nixon had already been undone from the other side by some of his Cuban supporters, the ones who had been caught putting tape on the Watergate doors.

To me, Miami Beach was an unlikely setting for political protest; the agitation was quite out of character for the state as I remembered it. Floridians, to my mind, were absorbers of enjoyment, preferring Thoroughbred handicapping and the demands of holing out in par to the demands of conscience. St. Petersburg, my childhood town, was a resort, and Miami Beach was a resort; people came to both to escape unpleasantness, Florida existed to obliterate our worldly cares. The Rebel cause was not the only cause on which one could lie down; in the decade of antiwar protests prior to the conventions of 1972, the most memorable Florida student demonstrations were the spring vacations in Ft. Lauderdale.

Even the amusements at the North Bay Road mansion were not typical Florida amusements as I recalled them: Cockette movies and platters of synthetic mescaline and sex with strangers in gauze pants were alien to the local entertainment formula of booze, bookies, and broads ordered up through the bellhops. I felt as if I had stumbled into Berkeley. Somehow, California had invaded Miami Beach.

California was the sister resort state to which the young Floridian had always made comparisons. Both had oranges, tourists, and sunshine; Florida, we thought, had better oranges and more sun. California had surfers that Florida's second-rate breakers could not support; Florida had divers and snorkelers. California had the movie stars; Florida the mermaids of Weekee Wachee. California had the rock musicians; Florida had Arthur Godfrey. California had the student riots; Florida had the collegiate spring revels. California was the psychedelic launching pad; Florida had Cape Canaveral.

California had the Beach Boys, Ken Kesey, Mario Savio, the Raymond Chandler novels; Florida had Jack Kerouac, come off the road to live with his mother in St. Petersburg, but Kerouac wasn't producing. California had definition, it had renewal; Californians were always struggling with something, as if they had ripped Manifest Destiny out of the geography books and swallowed it, internalizing the impulse that drove people West. Californians built up their bodies and crossed their biochemical divides in constant restlessness. What was the difference that made Florida, similar in setting, in oranges, in sunshine, the destination of traditional pleasure seekers, the apex of self-satisfaction?

The Floridian with a California complex was delighted at the news of every California mass murder. Whatever pushed them to turn out movie stars or rock musicians, fruititarians or clairvoyants, resisters and pamphleteers was suspected by Floridians to be the same force that made Charles Manson and Juan Corona. Better that we had the mermaids of Weekee Wachee and a general social sanity. Or if California didn't create its maniacs, certainly it imported them; the Florida schoolyard joke was that God tipped the continent on its side and shook it, and all the loose screws fell to the Pacific Coast.

Florida had its own famous murders, such as the Candy Mossler case, in which Mossler's young nephew was accused of hitting her sugar daddy banker over the head with a plaster flamingo so the two of them could get the sugar daddy's money, and then Candy and the nephew were acquitted. This Florida murder—whoever may have been responsible—had a concrete objective, as opposed to the Sharon Tate murder, which was bizarre and unfathomable, as bizarre and unfathomable as some of the people who occupied Miami Beach during the 1972 conventions.

I was the only inhabitant at the mansion with a Florida upbringing, and I was also the least comfortable person in the house. I became chauffeur to the mescaline takers, themselves too disoriented to drive. I adopted a Washington pose, continuing to dress in shirt, slacks, and tie, while the people around me did laps in distress over Southeast Asia. With my briefcase as my totem against the California enticements, I stood by the pool as if waiting to be rescued by a commuter train.

◆◆◆◆◆

I found myself standing by this pool once again, weeks and months beyond the convention, long after the other antidelegates had left. My coat and tie were hung in the closet; now I had a suntan. Something unexpected had occurred; Florida, with which I professed to share nothing in common, demanded my recall. I had returned to Washington, but only to settle accounts, finish work that I had promised, gather up belongings, and otherwise to disengage.

It was the reverse of the Thomas Wolfe predicament—the wanting to go home and then not finding it. Here I was moving back to Florida without ever having consciously desired it. The obvious cause of my transfer to Miami Beach was Susan, the best friend of the owner of the mansion. During the Republican event, Susan had been living in the round room upstairs. I had fallen in love with her. Never was I so smitten; she had been my link from the press corps, with which I still identified, to the mescaline corps, which I chauffeured around.

Susan was no Floridian. She came from New York, and more recently, from Nassau. She wore thin sarongs and had a voice like a lullaby from a dockworker. She was beautiful, quick-witted, and traveled with no suitcase. I took her for nineteen. Actually, she was thirty-four and had two children and a warehouse full of boxes. She could do the *New York Times* Sunday crossword.

We had decided to live together and we could have gone anywhere—back to her Manhattan or Nassau, or back to my Washington—yet we reunited on Miami Beach. Her children, her boxes, and a nanny joined me back at the mansion. For me, Susan and the house on North Bay Road were complementary attractions.

The deepest loyalties to one's childhood surroundings turn out to be visceral loyalties. It was visceral loyalty to Florida that once must have been established and now revived within me, loyalty to the moist air that irrigates the skin, to the humidity that excuses indolence, to the proximity of open water, to the midday heat in which corners of the buildings seem to vaporize, to the palm tree and the ficus, the hibiscus and the strangler fig, the North Bay Road camouflage.

Florida reached me through the pores and the eyes to awaken a subtropical disposition; it cleansed me of the self-important formality of Washington. Somehow, the surroundings had bypassed my mental block against the society they decorated. Perhaps that is the reason that I felt, during this transfer, as if some external force was controlling my destiny.

Is not the force that recalled me the eternal appeal of Florida? Since the beginning of its popularity, that is, since the 1880s, millions have come here not to be ennobled, awed, inspired, or moved to great works—what inventions, after all, does Florida claim beyond the air conditioner; what transcendence beyond poet Sidney Lanier, who wrote publicity pieces for the Florida railroads? Florida draws to different delight, its galvanic arousal of the human nerve endings as they charge in this sunlit openness, which suggests infinity, but being moisture-laden, simultaneously puts one to sleep.

"Here," Lanier wrote in 1875 in his *Florida, Its Scenery, Climate, and History,* "one has an instinct that it is one's duty to repose broad-faced upward, like fields in the fall, and to lie fallow under suns and airs that shed unspeakable fertilizations upon body and spirit. Here there develops itself a just proportion between quietude and activity: one becomes aware of a possible tranquillity that is larger than unrest."

No other state has quite this same effect, certainly not California, which after all is the apotheosis of the exertion that conquered the West. Florida offers an easier way out of things, and it was a sense of glorious recess from tedium that all the tropical plants, open water, and moist air evoked on my return. It was the same sense of recess that I first felt on the beaches of St. Petersburg, beachcombing, as a child.

Even after the convention was over, the mansion still contained numerous inhabitants. Visiting journalists stopped in from time to time; among the longer-term residents were people who professed to be boat captains, cooks, pilots, dancers, lawyers, but who rarely ventured outside. The open-door policy that let in all who agonized about Nixon was expanded to include those who knew someone who had agonized about Nixon. A multitude wandered in and out, staying a day, a week, a month; established guests got the bedrooms, relative newcomers slept downstairs on denim gym mats at the sides of the pool.

The place no longer reminded me of California: talk of politics was reduced to ritualistic babble, drugs were not taken with any sense of mission, they were more recreational than transcendental, even cocaine did not disturb the general lying around. By day, we floated in the pool and played backgammon; by night, we watched tiny and incompatible sea creatures fight it out in the invertebrate aquarium that was our substitute for television. With the passage of time, we became progressively debilitated, it got harder and harder to do anything but move from the bed to the backgammon table to the dinner table to the swimming pool and back again. Basic chores went undone, and because of the piles of dishes in the kitchen and the momentous refuse and people sleeping in all the rooms, the maids either ceased to function, imitating the residents, or else they quit.

One did not wander off the career path and into this house without some anxious self-analysis: why did I give up a good job in Washington for this? I wondered if a childhood in St. Petersburg, a retirement town, a reward for people who had struggled all their adult lives, had subtly prepared me for a precocious retirement, the way that a childhood in Montana might produce precocious ranchers, or a childhood in Maine might produce precocious lobstermen. I was only twenty-seven, opting for the swimming pool and the advantages of a senior citizen long before I had worked enough to deserve them. This was afterlife without the rigorous antecedents.

The owner supported us with her family trust fund. Our ultimate benefactor was her father, a former Philadelphia subdivision contractor who lived in a nearby Miami Beach condo and dropped in every week or so to survey the damage. We fancied ourselves as rebels from his system.

Susan, whose widow's bed I shared in the glorious round bedroom upstairs, had a big trust fund herself. From this charmed and yet unnerving vantage point, I looked back and concluded that a break with Washington was inevitable, that a latent subtropical disposition had retarded my potential for achievement even as a journalist in Washington. I could cite various examples of a lack of dedication; but whether it was a character flaw or a Florida trait I did not yet know. If the Watergate story, which was essentially a Florida story, had been assigned to a Floridian like me, it would still be a secret in the minds of the conspirators over on the other side of Biscayne Bay.

Whatever passed for enterprise in this sanitorium was regulated by the owner's boyfriend, the man with the beaded skullcap whom I had first met at the front door. His name was Bobby Gertz. He had a white beard and a five-foot-two frame; customarily, he wore a blue bandanna, and below that a white denim vest, no shirt, jeans, and little desert boots. In this outfit, he looked like a troll impersonating a gaucho. He expressed himself in aphorisms, such as "Eat now, you'll eat later."

Gertz carried a brown leather satchel to make himself appear businesslike, and he moved and talked as if he were in a great hurry. Every morning he would emerge from the bedroom with an exciting project: buying a restaurant, opening a hat store, getting a permanent booth at the flea market, leasing a movie house; by the afternoon each project would have been discarded. Apparently, this neglect at follow-through was not new; even before Gertz had become the boyfriend of the owner of the mansion he had organized a company that turned swimming pools into dance floors and back again into swimming pools, via a hydraulic platform called Aqualift, but Aqualift never got off the bottom. The mansion was full of inventory from other unrealized Gertz businesses: straw hats from Colombia, leather backgammon sets, wall hangings from Panama, discarded telephone booths. The living room resembled an Andean weekend bazaar.

Any time a resident took a Gertz proposal seriously enough to begin to work on it—for instance, by calling a local movie house and asking whether it might be leased—Gertz would counter by embellishing the proposal. "What's the point of having one movie house when we could open a string of movie houses?" he would theorize, until any further action became impossible. Then Gertz would challenge that resident to a game of backgammon. Killing an idea through embellishment we called "Gertzing the idea"; that is how entropy in the mansion was preserved. If one stayed here more than a few days, one learned that the goal of the mansion on North Bay Road was to preserve entropy while giving the illusion of productive activity.

For a time, I took the mansion as an antidote to Washington, reveling in my Hawaiian shirts, smug in my triumph over labor. After some months I began to despair that my residual dedication had no outlet. Gertz identified me as a retirement career failure. He could sense my discomfort with an aimless existence; if my latent subtropical disposition had sabotaged the will to work up North, here it was my latent will to work that sabotaged the capacity for enjoyment. To him, I was a foolish hybrid, a Calvinist in a bathing suit.

Every rule of behavior that I thought sensible or honorable was rejected by Gertz as dangerous or idiotic. In Washington, the first question asked at most gatherings is "Who are you with?"—or, if not that, then, "What do you do?" Washingtonians are comfortable neither with themselves nor with one another until their relative positions are fixed. At the mansion on North Bay Road, the idea was never to tell anybody what you did, and, if pressed, to make something up. Gertz himself was the champion at revealing nothing. I lived with my girlfriend, Susan, in the adjacent bedroom, a thin dividing wall away from him, and I spent perhaps eight or more hours a day in his company, yet it was a triumph to discover, after six months, that he had a mother who resided on Miami Beach. Gertz claimed that no photograph of himself existed; he would never give his right name even to a Sears deliveryman.

Gertz was neither shy nor quiet; it is only that he shared no information of value. Actually, he was a garrulous walking charade. His favorite activity, besides launching businesses with the half-life of a morning, was pretending to be somebody. In the front yard, he occasionally hacked at logs for a log cabin playhouse; passersby who saw him then would have sworn that he was an Amish penitent. I saw him pass himself off as an Israeli to a redneck and as a redneck to an Israeli. On the night of the arrival of the placebo comet Kohoutek, he wore a magician's costume and convinced half the people at Dinner Key Park that they had actually seen the thing. At the Democratic convention, Gertz had walked into the Fontainebleau Hotel lobby with such a managerial air that several workers followed his orders to take the huge official portrait of the Kennedys off the wall and put it in his car.

He set the tone for the rest of the house: other residents, who claimed to be pilots, cooks, dancers, lawyers, and so forth, turned out to be dissembling as well. Gradually, I discovered they shared another occupation that they hadn't mentioned to me, which, as the astute reader may have guessed by now, was not legal. They hadn't mentioned it because although I claimed to be a writer (in this setting any voluntary claim to an acceptable practice was assumed to be false) they suspected that I, too, had an occupation that I hadn't revealed: that of undercover narcotics agent.

Often, Gertz traveled to Colombia, but because of the restrictions of etiquette, or perhaps because of my suspected profession, it was impossible to know what he was really doing there. Sometimes I thought of all the straw hats and Andean products and flutter about movie houses as an elaborate front for the drug trade, sometimes I saw the drug trade as a front for his doing nothing and living off the trust fund. What could be cleverer than Gertz sneaking off to Medellín or Cali to preserve the image of derring-do that was the basis of his appeal with the owner of the mansion, and in fact bringing back nothing more exciting than the hats, which were a false front for the drugs, the drugs being a real front for the dole?

For the better part of a year, Susan and her two children and I stayed in the mansion under Gertz, among the transitory residents, with the widespread falsification of credentials, living indirectly off the retirement rewards of a builder from Philadelphia, rewards that may or may not have been augmented by the illegal supplementary income from halfhearted entrepreneurs who may have been selling hats or drugs and who pretended to organize retail stores. I have not emphasized the drugs, not only because I cannot prove Gertz's commercial involvement, but also because drugs were the least of Gertz's challenge to what I thought of as the rules of life. He represented more than a product, he represented a world view; his world was an extended midway of put-ons, where honesty was evidence not of good character but of mental retardation.

At the time, I would have sworn that the mansion was an aberration, that its philosophy and its etiquette would find few supporters outside the door. To me, Bobby Gertz was an interesting deviant whose teachings could be profitably applied only to carnivals, Mexican border stations, or to the import activities that at the time were still thought to be confined to small bands of coastal desperadoes. In the decade since then, I have reached a different conclusion—that what in my mind separated the mansion on North Bay Road from the rest of Florida were only myths of a Florida childhood. Unconsciously, I had returned to the right place.

Continental Drift

Where do you begin a book about a place? John McPhee introduced Alaska with his head in a trout stream, cooling his bandanna, we are on the Kitlik, the Salmon, admiring the works of nature, thank God, McPhee says, he isn't out there on a kayak.

Florida would seem to deserve a humbling first chapter, about how the place precedes us, the place will outlast us, the place is bigger than the impositions of man. It is famous for its natural assets, having been called such things as Nature's Greatest Wonder, Tropical Paradise, Promised Land, Land of Destiny, and when grammatical descriptions fail, inspiring mixed metaphors, such as Magnet Whose Climate Would Bring the Human Flood. It is the youngest part of the North American land mass, and the last part to emerge from the ocean. From *Land from the Sea,* a book written by marine geologist John Edward Hoffmeister and published by the University of Miami Press in 1974, we learn that the southern end sits in a huge porous bowl of limestone, made from the skeletons of billions of single-celled marine creatures, the bryozoans; and from the fusion of an even greater quantity of tiny mineral specks, the ooids, which under a microscope resemble roe.

How subtle Florida's emergence, as compared to the convulsions that produced the balance of the continent. The mass beneath us is the result of these microscopic toilers who did their work collectively and without fanfare, building up deposits on the underwater shelf, transforming themselves into the spongy, skeletal surface of the Florida bowl. While glacial slides and volcanic eruptions left canyons and mountains and other majestic residue around the world, Florida stayed underwater.

"Much of it is about as low as a place can be and still be called land," Hoffmeister described the state in his *Land from the Sea.* It was a geologic appendage forever amorphous, never quite earth, never quite ocean, raised up from the Atlantic and the Gulf of Mexico only to be dunked again with the melting and refreezing of the northern ice caps. The most recent and large-scale Florida emergence was during the Wisconsin Ice Age of less than 100,000 years ago. Florida was still waterlogged as man walked the solid ground of other regions, discovered fire, and learned to make tools.

Even as the limestone bowl broke the surface of the sea it never dried out entirely, and Florida's interior became a cavity for rainwater, filled with fertile muck, and aquatic vegetation, populated with birds, fish, and reptiles that had no impetus to evolve any further. The Florida travel diaries written by John and William Bartram and published in the late 1700s are full of descriptions of drenchings and soakings, and the only things that seemed to stick up out of Florida's lakes, rivers, bogs, and swamps with any regularity were the water plants and the snouts of alligators.

The Everglades is Florida's most famous remaining wilderness, and the advertisements for airboat rentals along Route 41, west of Miami, invite us to commune with it. Airboats are metal saucers with leather seats and DC-3 engines that spin across the swamps like skipping stones, just above the limestone in inch-deep water, and through the reeds that give this shallow sheet flow its name, "River of Grass." A better vehicle from which to contemplate Florida's prehistory could not be found, and yet, why bother to glorify Florida's geologic heritage, when geology is not responsible for Florida's final transformation into real estate?

It was this revelation that came to us in the heart of the waterlogged wilderness. Alaska may deserve McPhee's paean, but the lesson of the swamps teaches me that Florida's humbling forces merit only the courtesy of the above short mention, as opposed to the many pages I might otherwise have devoted to them.

In late 1973, we gathered up the two children and Susan's boxes from the warehouse, said goodbye to the mansion, and headed back to the land, away from Gertz, away from the threat of arrest or permanent stupor, away from a variety of actual and imagined predators, away from painful associations. It was during the period when young New York urbanites retreated to Vermont or New Hampshire, trading apartments with doormen for cabins with woodstoves, that we backed into rural Florida. Our Vermont was the Everglades, which to us was familiar as the emptiest spot on the Florida map.

Route 41 took us west, past the airport, past the orange-roofed subdivisions, where six lanes diminish to four, then four to two, the delicatessens give way to Cuban cafés and then to redneck barbecue, and even the barbecue is downgraded from pork or beef to gator tail as you get farther from the city, and finally all you see advertised is beer, ammo, and worms. Nowhere is evolutionary descent better symbolized than on this road. The terrain looks progressively rougher; the foliage scruffier; the Indian tourist villages, run by Pete

Osceola, then Joe Osceola, then Dan Osceola, more dilapidated.

The road is a dry strip that passes through a variety of inundations: the saltwater coastline to the south; the sawgrass plains grown up like wheat in the fields of standing freshwater to the north; the cypress bogs and sloughs that catch the fifty-five annual inches of rainfall; the rivulets and creeks where saltwater meets fresh and where the tannic acid from mangrove roots turns the runoff brown. Beyond Monroe Station, a rest stop for beer-ammo-worm patrons who drive swamp buggies; beyond the rock pits of Ochopee is the sign for Everglades City, eighty statute miles from Miami, and in less definable ways, more distant than that.

Everglades was a city only in name; no more than four hundred people lived here, mostly in ramshackle cottages built before World War II. The population was contained in a single square mile, there was a river on one side, a lake on the other, and in between were the houses, a hardware store, a malt shop, an old wooden hotel, a deteriorating stucco city hall, and the remains of the Captain's Table, a contemporary resort complex gone bankrupt, which served as a scarecrow for would-be entrepreneurs. A town never looked more bucolic to me.

The residents were third-generation Floridians, those native oddities outnumbered in south Florida most everyplace but here. These fishermen were friendly, polite, reserved, and straightforward; honesty did not seem to be a symptom of mental retardation with them. They waved at us from their pickup trucks and waved at each other with each pass—the town's one square mile supported wavers in constant motion. When they weren't waving from trucks, they were waving from their crab boats, which the men docked along the Barron River. The Barron River led through a bay and a labyrinth of small islands to the Gulf of Mexico.

When they returned from fishing or from retrieving stone-crab traps out in the Gulf, the men docked their boats along the river and behind the seafood companies. They stacked their traps up on the banks. Between the traps and the nets, the discarded outboard motors and the little wooden cottages, the north end of town looked like one of those marine collages found on the walls of raw bars.

Everglades City was two towns, really. On the north end was the local's town, and on the south end the Yankee's town where a few modern houses were put up on stilts and well maintained by a minority of misanthropic retirees. The retiree's efforts at lawn care did not overcome the general seediness, the high grass in empty lots unmowed during the rainy season, the streets full of potholes, the crooked sabal palms, fifty feet tall, standing like anorexic sentinels around an old white stucco building, left over from the 1920s. The town centerpiece was a gigantic microwave tower, symbol of fealty to the local phone company, and below it were two phone booths decorated like Hawaiian huts, which served as collection jars for the swarms of mosquitoes.

We bought a lot on this south end and prepared to build a genuine Florida house, with no air-conditioning, porches on two sides, paddle fans, open to nature's breezes, and with a view of the Barron River. It was here, engaged in back-to-the-land activities, such as making sea grape wine and debarking cypress pilings with primitive two-handled draw knives, constructing a fish smoker, fantasizing about subsistence, that we learned we were homesteading on a failed golf course. Before it was a golf course, it was a tidal mangrove swamp. Exclude a stretch of high ground along the riverbank, and there was not a legitimate acre of earth in Everglades City. The Barron River had been artificially diverted. The lake on the opposite boundary was the result of a big hole, scooped out of the swamps by a machine; the contents of the scoops were dumped onto the adjacent swamplands to raise them above water; 80 percent of the real estate was dredged up; 80 percent of the town's surface man-made.

It was here, in the middle of the Everglades, that our respect for Florida as a geologic wonder was challenged by the fact that neither Genesis nor geology was directly responsible for the ground underneath our feet. There was a layer of limestone a fathom or so below our property, no doubt the result of bryozoans or ooids piling up their dead, but it would have taken aeons for the ooids to reach the level of dry land, the level at which we stood. Giving credit where credit is due, it only took the dredges a few weeks.

We first learned the identity of the local creator from place mats at the old wooden hotel, the Rod and Gun Club. His name was Barron G. Collier, which explains the name of the river. Collier, born in Memphis in 1873, was a stern-looking aristocrat: in the lobby of the Rod and Gun, just above the pool table and to the left of the alligator skin, there was a picture of Collier in a starched shirt, peering out from among various stuffed fish with Teutonic disdain.

Collier was an adman whose career began in a Memphis print shop that made flyers to be stuck to the sides of horse-drawn streetcars. From Memphis, he traveled the country, picking up exclusive franchises on the placard rights to subways, trolleys, and public buses in many major cities, building a monopoly in overhead spaces that nobody else wanted. In Chicago, New York, New Orleans, straphangers were entertained with Collier's ads, and Collier was rewarded with millions. He took his first Florida vacation in 1911 on an island off the coast near Ft. Myers. By the 1920s, he was dredging and platting Everglades City. Even in the remotest of habitats, one runs into a developer.

◆◆◆◆◆

The Barron River had Collier's first name, the county had his last; our fishing village had been his company town, dug up and platted by his engineers, populated by his employees, financed by his bank. The old stucco buildings were all Collier buildings, erected in the 1920s, the city sewer plant and the water plant were originally the Collier utilities, the older men whom we saw cleaning their traps along Collier's river were ex-Collier fishing guides.

Sam Bonard, who slept in a trailer behind the gas station and by day circled the town alone in his car, was once the captain of a Collier dredging crew that built Route 41—also called the Tamiami Trail—across the Everglades. The Tamiami Trail was Collier's road, his dynamite crews blasted and loosened the oolitic rock, and his giant shovel machines followed behind, scooping and piling the rubble into the two-lane passage, raised a few inches above the surrounding wetlands. It cost Collier several million dollars to complete this highway, a feat that was equated with the digging of the Panama Canal.

It was not only in his company town that Collier's word was law; between 1921 and 1923 the placard magnate purchased one million acres, 5 percent of the southern two-thirds of the peninsula, making him the largest landowner in the state. For 20 miles in each direction, west and south along the coastline, north and east along Route 41, everything had been his. The legislature in 1923 redrew the political boundaries to give Collier the county, not simply to gratify his ego, but to enable him to control local affairs. He picked his own officials, most importantly the tax assessors. He owned both regional newspapers, published from Naples and from Ft. Myers. Collier was more than a neighborhood developer; we had happened onto his Florida monarchy, awarded in the twentieth century.

Collier was an absentee monarch, visiting Everglades City

only infrequently from his yacht, the *Baroness.* His subordinates administrated from the stucco building that served as the county seat. The Tamiami Trail was supposed to bring the tourists, the vacationers, the land buyers. Anticipating the crowds, Collier's aides chartered a steamship company, a telephone company, the Trailways bus company, and a mercantile company. They designed the town around a central hub, with boulevards of Parisian width, wide enough for all the traffic that would be enticed. Collier had planned to build another hotel near his golf course, the same golf course over which we were now simplifying our lives.

In 1973, the year of our arrival, the old county building—now the Everglades city hall—had the look of a dowager lost in high grass. It did not take many offices to govern a town of four hundred, and most of the space was devoted to the storage of sewer pipe and two-by-fours. Collier's Parisian hub extended out for a few blocks and then abruptly terminated in patched-up single lanes. Collier lost his fortune in the Great Depression, his Florida development did not succeed, what we took for our unspoiled retreat was his overgrown inventory, our pantheism had venerated his civil engineers.

An awareness of our local creator caused us to view the Everglades in general with a different eye. In all the miles of inundation, the only dry ground was in places where machines had scooped it up, either in Collier's resort town or along the sides of his road. There was a neighboring village of Chokoloskee Island, which rose to thirty feet above sea level in its interior, and this was not Collier's project, but even Chokoloskee was a human development of sorts, a thirty-foot mound of shucked oyster shells, piled up over generations by the Calusa Indians.

Readers of geographic magazines are encouraged to think

of the Everglades as distinctive habitat—and it is distinctive in certain subtle ways—but basically, the Everglades is pre-dredged Florida real estate. Not that Collier would have filled it all in—even in the 1920s there were plans to preserve certain sections. But absent his financial collapse and his death in 1939, and absent his heirs' donation of hundreds of square miles to the Everglades National Park, the coastline along this lower west coast might easily have gone the way of Miami Beach. In fact, Miami Beach and Everglades City were more or less contemporary projects.

The tourist who drives out here from his condominium in Miami Beach or Sarasota, thinking that he is in unique territory, may not realize that Miami Beach and Sarasota were just as wet as the wet Everglades, and in very recent times. Look at old photographs of Miami in 1920, or of the coastline of St. Petersburg in 1930, and you see the same aquatic forests of mangrove trees, their roots stuck in the tides, that we saw around Everglades City in 1973. In the interior of the state, and as recently as the advent of talking movies, half the property south of Orlando could only have been called "land" during the winter dry season.

The drying of swamp is where Florida begins, at least the part of Florida that we recognize, the southern part where the real estate is now priceless, the part that half the country thinks of as its final destination. Swamp is what preserved Florida for so long against the country's progress. Two hundred and fifty years after the landing of the Pilgrims, 150 years after the establishment of major American cities, 100 years after the western migrations, 75 years after the Civil War, the balance of Florida was separated from civilization by water, not an impassable and violent river, but a thin and inclusive sheet that covered its limestone bowl.

In the span of a contemporary lifetime, Florida was elevated by dredges, elevated from post-Pleistocene aqueous directly to retirement subdivision without an epoch in between.

Nature's wonder it was in theory, paradise in the literature of the land barons, but paradise conditional on the mechanical uplift. In practice, Florida was extraordinarily devalued, first as a whole and then in part; devaluation is what made it possible for a Barron Collier, rich but no Rockefeller, to pick up one million Florida acres at a time when a thousand Florida acres elsewhere would have cost as much or more. Swamp is what Collier bought; swamp is why this second-string magnate, who controlled the air space above the strap-hangers but who did not own the trains, could gain a Florida monarchy. Forty years before Collier purchased the lower southwest coast he could have had the St. Petersburg coast, and for an equally low price. Worthless became priceless on the scoop.

Collier's purchase is a minor consequence of Florida's internal disparagement. One only has to go back to the 1850s to find two-thirds of the land mass, or 24 million acres, designated "swamp and overflowed" or "wet and unfit for cultivation" by the federal government itself. This wholesale rejection encompassed large sections of dry and usable high ground, barrier island beaches, hammocks, and bluffs, even some of the hills that now support orange groves between Orlando and Lake Okeechobee.

Florida's entire population by 1880 was only 260,000, and all but a handful lived north of Orlando, atop geologic humps that raised the land above the level of bryozoans and ooids, amidst hills and oak trees and plantation surroundings, a suitable background for the Confederate posturing with which the state as a whole is mistakenly associated. Neo-Floridians who had descended from Georgia and the Carolinas were as unfamiliar with subtropical conditions as any contemporary tourist, and from the state's capital city, Tallahassee, they contemplated the lower regions that would produce the most expensive real estate in the world as one might contemplate gangrene.

"Swamp and overflowed," the justification for the federal government having given away the 20 million-plus acres to the state, later was the state's justification for giving away the same millions of acres to any private parties who proposed to correct the defect. Various governors and legislators offered free land to hastily chartered railroad companies, carpetbaggers, inventors, and insolvents—anybody who promised to drain the lower regions and connect them to the upper regions with trains.

A government giveaway of giant parcels of real estate is not unusual in American history; that is how the railroads won the West. But the early Florida land deals were struck in a particular desperation, in which state officials not only awarded free acres to railroads and would-be dredgers, but—believing Florida acres to be insufficient inducement—also financed the dredging or the laying of the track. Even then, the railroad companies and would-be dredgers usually went bankrupt after they relieved the high ground of timber and other marketable assets. The state land fund, which had backed the railroads with bonds, nearly went bankrupt as well.

An investigation of Collier's purchase takes us back to this formative period, the period of the first dredgers. The state is fiscally stuck in its own morass, public servants unable to cull fact from fantasy from among the various Rube Goldbergs peddling schemes to pull the Florida plug. Trustees of the land fund try to save it from bankruptcy the only way they know how, by deeding additional millions of acres to new railroad companies, until by the 1880s more than 60 percent of the entire state was owned by five railroad enterprises, one drainage outfit, and Hamilton Disston.

The Florida Statement of Swamp Lands, January 1, 1883, is as follows:

BALANCE ON HAND	14,754,361 acres
SALES OR GRANTS	
Pensacola and Atlantic Railroad	3,200,000 acres
Okeechobee Drainage Lands	1,781,051 acres
Florida Southern Railroad	4,000,000 acres
Jacksonville–Tampa–Key West Railroad	3,000,000 acres
Palatka and Indian River Railroad	1,500,000 acres
Sales to Settlers	26,690 acres
Hamilton Disston	4,000,000 acres
TOTAL SOLD OR GRANTED	17,507,741 acres

Florida land was considered so unworthy even of measurement or careful survey that the governors and legislatures had given away 2,753,380 more acres than existed in fact. Hamilton Disston got a most generous real parcel; in 1881, he walked out of Tallahassee with the south-central core in his pocket, taking enough of the peninsula from St. Petersburg to Lake Okeechobee to make him instantly the largest single property holder in the United States and one of the largest in the world.

Disston, known as "Ham," was the gregarious son of a Philadelphia saw manufacturer, famous for his Florida stag fishing parties—stag fishing with rich Republicans. He invested in their campaigns. Like the inhabitants of the mansion on North Bay Road, Disston lived off his father's business, most of his attention devoted to the pursuit of happiness and the contemplation of projects too grandiose for any reasonable preparation. Once, he had volunteered to dredge up a small parcel around Lake Okeechobee, and when that project ran into legal complications, he Gertzed the idea by including the lower trunk of Florida as a whole.

He shared his scheme with then-Governor William Bloxham, a stag fishing enthusiast himself, and the result was that Bloxham's administration sold Disston 4 million acres, 10 percent of the state land mass, for 25 cents an acre. With this $1 million, the state could gain back some solvency and liberate even more acreage from old railroad creditors, acreage that would be private industry's fee for draining the swamps.

Disston, meanwhile, did not have the $1 million, nor did he have a dredge. The nation has periodically asked great capitalists like J. P. Morgan for financial assistance, and frequently it has relied on great scientists and inventors for technical assistance, but one can only marvel at Florida's choice of Disston as its last and greatest hope. What better evidence of Florida's self-perceived inferiority, its hat-in-hand attitude, its inability to distinguish substance from pose, its susceptibility to bluster in the infancy of its statehood than this 1881 Disston deal.

Almost before he had pocketed the deeds, Disston packaged about half of his new possession for quick resale and used that money to cover most of his $1 million debt to the state. He was left with 2 million acres that cost him next to nothing, some of it high and dry. To drain the rest, he ordered the manufacture of two huge machines, and shipped them down on barges to dig ruts from Lake Okeechobee to the Gulf coast and up the Kissimmee River. The rutting was successful in some spots, but more ballyhooed than effective at large.

The prospect of transforming the earth's surface excited Disston, he knew that Nature's Wonder in its processed form would someday be irresistible. He opened Florida land sales offices in every major U.S. city and even in Europe, but Disston was victimized by the financial panic of 1893.

Insolvent after that panic, Disston committed suicide in Philadelphia. He shot himself as he lay in his bathtub, at least ending his life with a successful drainage there. His heirs, agreeing with Florida's leaders about the uselessness of the property now in their possession (why else would so much of it have been handed over to their party-loving relative?), sold it off for less than the 25 cents an acre that Disston had contracted to pay.

Barron Collier's 1 million acres, which surrounded us from Everglades City, was a paltry empire as compared to Disston's 4 million. Collier's acres were acquired forty years later, but as a result of the same depreciation; old railroad and timber companies, once granted the swamps for nothing, had stripped them of cypress and were willing to sell cheap.

The existence of that few inches of water over so much of Florida's surface had a profound effect on the character of its colonizers. Florida was a land of dreams, as every new territory is, but at first it could not attract those great numbers of little dreamers who out of hard work and simple expectations create prosperity. Little dreamers carried timber axes across the Appalachians and the Great Plains, but they could not have carried dredges across Florida. In the huge grants listed above, only 26,690 acres were alloted to settlers. South of Orlando, Florida was opened up in the nearly-exclusive control of big dreamers: admen, saw manufacturers, capitalists who acquired huge chunks wholesale. Frequently, the owners were of as uncertain substance as the real estate they held.

Is Florida the last American frontier? Every state and region has made such a claim during one period or another. American scholar Frederick Jackson Turner saw a succession of frontiers, first along the New England borders, then along the Piedmont, the Appalachians, the Mississippi, the Great Lakes, the Rockies, the Pacific Coast. By the time Turner gave his lecture to the American Historical Association in 1893, suggesting that the last wilderness had been reached,

Hamilton Disston had gained and was about to lose his 4 million empty Florida acres.

Across to California went the pathfinders, followed by trappers and vagabonds, farmers and bridge builders, and finally bankers and the sellers of silks, pianos, and European furniture. Along the Florida frontier, pickled in standing water, the bankers and decorators came first, and save for a handful of rowdies and ruddy eccentrics, the developers were the pioneers. Florida was tamed in reverse—the Colliers of the state imposing their roads, landscaping, plats, and fancy hotels before the people arrived. South Florida began as a collection of wholly owned utopias connected to cash registers. I doubt if there is a greater percentage of such predestined communities in any other region of the world.

If Collier was no Rockefeller, then Disston was no Collier; that so much of Florida could be had by either of them is a measure of the extent to which the entire state was up for grabs.

So our homesteading on Collier's fill project in Everglades City was no ironic exercise. It was the only way a nominal Floridian could truly go back to his land. In the late 1950s and early 1960s, I spent my childhood on a pie-shaped lot on Redington Beach, a suburb of St. Petersburg. Geology deserves no credit for its appearance, either. Hindsight suggests that my father could have contracted the manufacture of the property himself, instead of buying retail, but he was a schoolteacher, lacked capital, and had a respect for immutable earth that must have come from his earlier experience in Minnesota, Illinois, and Connecticut.

For four years, we rented a house in an established section of Redington Beach, a Gulf-front community of functional concrete rectangular houses with terrazzo floors. We were four blocks from the beach. There were no high-rises to mar the view. The biggest hotel in the area had, I think, five stories.

St. Petersburg was on the mainland, and we reached it by crossing a causeway and a drawbridge. It was a sizable city. Except for one or two famous dips in certain streets, St. Petersburg and its satellite communities were built on ground as flat as the water's surface.

We saved up to buy a new lot in a fresh section, dredged out of Boca Ciega Bay. The local manufacturer was a neighbor of ours named Jack Holton. Holton understood the Florida process. He could see through the statement "They aren't making any more"; he knew that every deed to every piece of waterfront real estate in Florida carried a riparian provision, as important to Floridians as the right not to pay taxes. The riparian provision allowed landowners to extend the existing lot lines into the water as far out as the bulkhead—usually set at the edge of navigable channels—and then to fill between the lines with muck scooped up from another part of the bay. This transfer of sediment was also a triumph of capitalism; the public bay bottom would reemerge as private property.

Much of the Florida interior was dried out by the 1950s, the rainfall and the sheet flow diverted through an elaborate system of culverts and dams installed by the Army Corps of Engineers. But there was still dredging on the coastlines; the Florida waterfront was a dynamic reproductive culture in which a small bit of substance could produce more. The Florida waterfront, in that sense, was less like land than like yoghurt.

Holton's starter culture came in the form of waterfront lots on Redington Beach, sold to him cheaply because the owners had been feuding. Eastward from these two lots across Boca Ciega Bay, he could dredge for about a mile until he was impeded by a channel. He was required to leave some open water between the old lots and the new ones to ensure that the earlier property would not be gradually landlocked by later reproduction, losing its connection with the bay. Florida coastal fills that seem to blob out at the ends of long, thin causeways are shaped that way for the protection of the previous waterfront.

As consumers of a Holton lot, we were not very appreciative of the effort that we witnessed. We could have watched the dredging, but we didn't pay particular attention, dredges were as routine as seagulls in Boca Ciega Bay, as routine but more discredited. Inhabitants of each successive fill would count themselves as opponents of further filling, the Gulf coast was full of residents who lived on dredged land and regarded themselves as enemies of the process.

Recently, and with the help of our family dredger, who still lives on Gulf Boulevard in Redington Beach, I have reconstructed the event that the revelation in the Everglades gave more universal importance. Holton was a small-scale practitioner of an art that can be traced back to the Fertile Crescent, back to the Tigris and the Indus flood plains, back to Nebuchadrezzar, who sent his people out with buckets to scoop a new path for the Euphrates; back to Darius, who ordered the digging of a rut to connect the Nile with the Red Sea; back to Assryian king Sennacherib, who made canals to Nineveh; then forward to the spade and baskets used by the soldiers of Claudius to scoop the ports of Italy; forward to the bag and spoon contraptions that first drained the Netherlands; to the hand drags of Gaul; to the mud mill, the grab dredge, the agitation dredge, the scrapper, scraper, plow, and mole, the centrifugal pump dredge, and on to the draglines and suction dredges that the nominal Floridian can thank for the very foundation of his adolescent existence, now anchored in Boca Ciega Bay and spewing out our homestead.

The dredging equipment was floated over from Tampa on two huge barges. Sections of concrete seawall were lowered into the water with a crane from one of the barges. The seawall defined the territorial boundaries of the new property. From the other barge, a long pipe was extended into the water, like a hose on a vacuum, to suck up the bay bottom outside the seawall. The leading end of the pipe was fitted with a special attachment, called a cutter, to loosen and pulverize the sediment. The cutter was connected to a crane, an operator could move it around from inside the barge.

The silt and muck was drawn through the cutter and into the pipe, then pumped along the full length of the barge and spilled out of a discharge line and into the seawall mold. When the muck had filled up the mold, a tractor was driven across it, slitting the surface the way one slits a pie crust, so the excess liquid could ooze out from below. The mound was leveled and lot lines drawn on the top. Holton was required by law to delay settlement for at least a few weeks in order to give the real estate time to solidify. Otherwise, it might fall in.

After we became occupants of the newly solidified 163rd Street finger fill, we still believed that most of the adjacent earth had impersonal origins, even in 1956 there was a confusion between geology and the civil engineers. My father, usually well-informed, assumed that the interior of Redington Beach, where we had rented a house before purchasing a Holton lot, was naturally high ground. Holton, during my recent visit to him, told me that it, too, was dredged back in the 1930s, by a John Redington, who got the idea from D. P. Davis over in Tampa. Davis had filled in an island in the early 1920s and sold $3 million worth of lots in a single day, then later was murdered at sea while taking some of his profits on an ocean cruise. (The shipboard story that he committed suicide by squeezing himself through a porthole strains credulity.)

D. P. Davis, Holton said, got the land-making idea from Carl Fisher. The name was familiar, I had heard it in 1972 during my Florida reentry. Carl Fisher was the developer of Miami Beach, North Bay Road was built on his fill, the concrete minaret visible from our poolside, just beyond the Cockette movie, was an out-building for Fisher's former house.

The Floridian learns of Florida's makers in accidental ways: Barron Collier was introduced on a placemat in Everglades City; Carl Fisher's faded photograph was unceremoniously hung in a Miami Beach branch post office like a snapshot that a neighbor had tacked up. Fisher wore tiny glasses out of scale with the rest of him, his face grew through his glasses like a bubble blown through a bubble pipe. Under the picture was a framed typewritten page, written by Fisher's wife, Jane, which read:

> Carl Graham Fisher was born on January 12, 1874, in Greensburg, Indiana, and died July 15, 1939 in St. Francis Hospital, Miami Beach. He was forced to leave school at 12 years of age because of his 50 per cent vision which made it impossible for him to see the blackboard. Teachers figured him a dunce and he won the nickname "Crip" because he often stumbled and fell. Beginning with nothing, he built a vast business and sold it for $10 million. He gave Presto-O-Light compressed gas lanterns to the world . . . the first lighting for the automobile. . . . He filed his first realty holdings in Miami on January 15, 1914, and pumped in three million cubic yards of dirt from the bottom of Biscayne Bay to make the land on which Miami Beach is built. . . . As he said, "the most beautiful city in the world."

Collier to Holton to Davis and now back to Carl Fisher; Miami Beach, Everglades City, and Redington Beach had this underlying compatibility. At one level, they were indebted to the ooids, at another, to the Indiana salesman, Fisher, the first coastal reclaimer; and, like Noah, the importer of all forms of life to his artificial land.

Surroundings

Does Carl Fisher deserve to be remembered as the father of Florida? Certainly, he was not its earliest developer, having arrived in Miami for the first time in 1913, or thirty years after Hamilton Disston had tried to drain and peddle his countless acres. Nor was he the most prolific; that honor belongs unquestionably to Henry Flagler, Rockefeller's expert on freight kickbacks, who bought up the bankrupt railroads and extended them from Jacksonville to Key West, opening the first snazzy hotels in Daytona, Palm Beach, Miami, and rescuing the entire east coast of the state from chronic devaluation. Flagler lured more crowds to Florida than all the previous promoters combined. Miami had only 257 inhabitants before he arrived there; St. Augustine, 2,000.

Flagler is exemplary not only for what he did to Florida, but also for what the state did to him. He was a glorious receptacle for the Florida spirit that has infused shopkeepers and bureaucrats, as well as robber barons, ever since his day. Having just married the nurse of his recently deceased wife, and looking for a forum to celebrate this rejuvenation, this pious Presbyterian arrived with his bride in St. Augustine in

1883. It was exceptionally warm in St. Augustine and also cold in New England that year, and the newlyweds stayed the winter and beyond the winter, mesmerized in the unseasonable balm, charmed by local historical pageants put on by Seminole Indians.

Flagler was 53, a multi-millionaire, and hoping to relax. But so many capitalists, large and small, come here ostensibly to rest but then cannot resist the fantastic prospect that is paraded before them. Florida turns the most confirmed seekers of peace and quiet into reborn speculators in shell shops, motels, restaurants, condominiums, and in Flagler's case, the entire Atlantic coast. After one winter of relaxation, he devoted the next to the construction of a fantastic new resort, and soon he was consumed by Florida, pulled farther south, gathering land, dredging, founding cities, constructing more and better accommodations, until finally he reached Key West. He transported settlers with him, and the first settler's outpost in each successive instance was neither a trading post nor a fort, but a Flagler hotel.

Like the multitude that followed him, Flagler was loosened up by Florida, inspired by the lack of impediment to unreasonable endeavor, until finally he was boggled by a woman half his age. In 1901, Flagler's trains had reached below Miami, Flagler had reached 70 years, and his second wife—who once nursed the first—had gone hopelessly insane. Insanity was no grounds for divorce in Florida, not until Flagler got a new law passed through both houses of the Florida legislature and signed by the governor in less than a month. His third bride, whom he married 11 days after the divorce was granted, was 34.

Flagler is a father figure, but it is still Carl Fisher, neither the earliest nor the most prolific developer, who merits a greater deference. Fisher, whose likeness I first saw in the post office, took the Florida land-making process to its logical and most spectacular end. Why not start civilization entirely from scratch?

Back at the time of the Disston grant, Fisher was just a boy in Indiana with a knack for salesmanship. As a preadolescent, he stimulated newspaper sales by wearing a smock with a naked lady painted on the fabric; as a teenager, he stimulated bicycle sales by riding across a tight wire suspended between the two tallest buildings in Indianapolis; as a twenty-five-year-old, he stimulated car sales by floating over that city in the newest model, hung like a basket beneath a vermilion balloon.

Despite his terrible eyesight, Fisher raced every kind of vehicle he sold. With Barney Oldfield as his companion, he competed on the ground in cars and bicycles and above it in balloons and airplanes, bouncing around America like a heated molecule. He built the Indianapolis speedway, organized the first national highway, and bought a patent for gas headlights, which made him a millionaire just in time for the opening up of lower Florida, the new millionaire's playground.

Americans at the turn of the century had already moved from farms to cities, and many were reverting to nature, to the landscaped and pacified suburban habitats where animals were declawed and trees were pruned and where land did not have to produce income. A whole class of literary commuters took to bird-watching and gentlemanly country pastimes: they read the Lake poets; they cited the Romantics; they admired the paintings of Rousseau, who after all got his jungle scenes from the Paris zoo. Now they could come to Florida, still a frontier in the sense that it was uninhabited, but colonized in the suburban spirit; Florida, the postindustrial Arcadia, perfectly romantic as an ideal, perfectly dreadful until remade.

The ritual of seasonal repose had passed from the New

England aristocracy to nouveau riche midwesterners like Fisher, as it would eventually pass to secretaries, truck drivers, short-order cooks, and sanitation workers. Seasonal repose was an obligation of the wealthy, a winter in Florida was a necessary proof of wealth, in conspicuous consumption of time. Florida could not yet support year-round retirement, that final proof of wealth, because there were no air conditioners.

By 1913, Fisher had made enough money on his auto headlights to send his yacht to Miami and ride down to meet it on Henry Flagler's railroad. His peers in Miami stayed one or two months, in mansions or in fancy hotels perched on pads of dry ground above the mangroves and along the coastal flood plain. One of his neighbors was the owner of the cough-drops, met each season by brass bands and velvet carpets to carry him across bogs to the entranceway of his house, which was emblazoned in neon lights flashing: "Ludens."

With nothing better to do, Fisher bounced a speedboat around Miami's Biscayne Bay, where he ran into Miami Beach. Miami Beach consisted of a beach on the eastern side, then an elongated bluff where a Quaker named Collins tried to grow avocadoes, then acres and acres of mangrove roots covered at high tide on the west. Fisher had been introduced to the dredge by a neighbor of his named Locke Highleyman, who contrived a suction machine to amplify the square footage of his own backyard on the Miami waterfront. Highleyman had the technique, but Fisher had the perspective. With an inspiration that must have resulted from his struggle against boredom, Fisher took Highleyman's dredge and the Quaker's tidal swamp and applied the one to the other.

Miami Beach is the founding example of what happened along both Florida coasts. Once the dredges corrected the basic defect, developers were left with a tabula rasa of dried silt, as empty and devoid of precedent as an atoll after a nuclear strike. Where has there been a more convenient opportunity to remodel the surroundings than Florida in the modern age? Europe was made over, but that took centuries. Upper America was partially made over, but its pioneers had to suffer in the wilderness for years before they could eliminate it. As Turner said in his frontier lecture: "The wilderness masters the colonist . . . the frontier environment is at first too strong for the man. He must accept the conditions it furnishes, or perish."

Even after the American forests were cut there were mountains or canyons and other impediments to chasten the most ardent believer in the supremacy of mankind. Not in Florida. Florida was flat, with no superficial obstacles, no geologic barriers to human aspirations. Out on Miami Beach, Fisher's machines eliminated every bird, every bush, every tree, every knoll, every scrap of vegetation. Miami Beach emerged flat and clean as a wafer, slipped between the sky and the sea.

The favorable Florida climate and new methods of horticulture made it possible to impose an eclectic landscape, gathered and installed outdoors. Fisher's hero was the agnostic Republican Robert Ingersoll, who elevated man's industrial achievements to the level of religion. The developer, who also believed in the superiority of the man-made product, assembled his resort like a bicycle, a car, or an airplane, parts coming from everywhere but Miami Beach.

The grass was from Bermuda, planted sprig by sprig from baskets hung on the backs of Bahamian migrants. For trees and shrubs there were Arabian jasmine, Brazilian pepper, Australian pine, Chinese holly, Canary Island date palm, Hong Kong orchids, Mexican flame vine, Rangoon creeper, Surinam cherry, and the gardeners were Japanese. Gondoliers brought in from Venice pushed boats up and down

Fisher's man-made Venetian canals. Local birds abandoned the area after their mangrove rookeries were destroyed, but more colorful substitutes arrived in crates—flamingoes were snared from Bimini by poachers and when those birds died, replacement flamingoes were shipped from Africa; peacocks shipped from Asia; geese from Canada; along with pheasants to decorate Fisher's polo fields. Polo fields required polo ponies, and those coexisted with honey bears, singing seals, and an elephant named Rosie, trained by a Georgia sharecropper named Yarnell.

The buildings were as new to Florida as the imported flora and fauna. What we call the Florida style was imposed by architects who ignored the airy houses with the wide overhangs and the cupolas for upper ventilation, constructed by the few predeveloper pioneers, in favor of massive stucco dwellings, some of them heat traps in which paintings, draperies, and correspondence could mold up as quickly as old bread.

The Florida-Spanish style had nothing to do with the Spanish colonizers. The first Moorish castle in Florida was not built by a Moor, but by a migratory Bostonian named Franklin W. Smith. Smith's St. Augustine home was a poured Arabian battlement, the Villa Zorayda, completed circa 1882. The Bostonian's Iberian villa is what influenced Henry Flagler, who bought up the bankrupt railroads and dropped the hotels along his line, to popularize the Spanish theme. Flagler's original Florida hotel, the Ponce De Leon of St. Augustine, had a sort of Moorish body with Renaissance limbs and dominated the city like a major church, only to be challenged by another hotel built by Smith, the source of the Moorish inspiration, who this time upstaged Flagler's Renaissance limbs with medieval turrets. What fun it was. Addison Mizner, Flagler's architect at Palm Beach, had a profound effect on the Florida style, and after he was done with it, it looked more Italian than Spanish. Mizner is said to have cribbed his Florida vision from pictures of Italian façades he ripped from European art books, and also from the illustrations of books by Sir Walter Scott.

Carl Fisher's most famous Miami Beach hotel, the Flamingo, was a Spanish-Moorish building, therefore a product of Boston influence and perhaps of English illustration. It was named for a bird that no longer existed in Florida and had to be kidnapped from Bimini. Its guests took rides on Venetian canals, bathed in Roman pools, and watched polo matches played on fields stippled with Asian fowl. The rival development of Opa-Locka had minarets guarded by ersatz Arabs on white horses; Coral Gables had Chinese and French villages erected along its Italian waterways; up in Boca Raton, Wilson Mizner, brother of the architect, Addison, installed electric gondolas and imported gondoliers, and, when told that gondoliers weren't needed for the propulsion, he said: "Let them pretend to row."

In Coral Gables, Eau Gallie, Boca Raton, Miami Beach, Disston City, and many sections of Ft. Myers, Sarasota, and St. Petersburg, the tabula rasa was pumped up, the flora from elsewhere took root, wildlife was shipped in for diversion.

There was a Florida hubris, and Carl Fisher is an early but typical example of it. Developers believed their invented landscape would attract not only humans, but also all the birds and animals they originally displaced, not to mention various alien birds and animals who would learn of the improvements and migrate here of their own volition. Because of Fisher's glorification of flamingoes, most visitors thought flamingoes still belonged on Miami Beach, even though it was dredged up and denuded of rookeries. It was only one step from that delusion to the hopeful sentiment expressed by Fisher himself on the front page of a 1930 *Miami News:*

FISHER TELLS HOW FLAMINGO MAY COME BACK

Carl Fisher is a great lover of nature. To a few of his friends, he has issued the following communication on the subject of conserving bird life here: "Thousands of flamingoes, cranes, and ducks used to inhabit the shores of Biscayne Bay. With the coming of the dredges that were so active for years, filling in the land all along the bayfront, these beautiful waterfowl were driven away from here. You can have many of these wild birds come right to your waterfront home if you want them. We have hundreds of them at the Flamingo Hotel every winter now, and here's how you can attract them to your place: tie a small line to a board that is about eight inches wide, two inches thick, and two or three feet long. On this board tie a loaf of whole wheat or rye bread; never use white bread, as that will kill the birds; let this board drift out 50 or 100 feet and pull it in each day or two, depending on how rapidly the bread is eaten. The birds may not discover this food for several days, but once they do, you can depend upon it that you will have them with you in increasing numbers."

In 1973, Everglades City still showed signs of Collier's attempts at importation of forms: the sabal palms now so tall they had outgrown the local picture, the tracks of his ceremonial Chicago trolley still sunk in the roadbed, the Parisian hub, the Spanish-stucco city hall with its Greek façade, the foundation of the cage where the South American monkeys were kept. Clearly, it was a case of arrested development. Wilderness had retaken the town, reclaimed Collier's fantasy. His little village, plus the mound of oyster shells piled thirty feet high under the neighboring community of Chokoloskee, were pathetic examples of Florida hubris when compared to the hundreds of square miles of Everglades in our backyard.

We built our house on stilts. Everything in Everglades City had been built on stilts, eight feet above road grade, since

1960, when Hurricane Donna flooded the town to seven feet six inches. The next hurricane might flood up to ten feet, but at least we were prepared for the last.

The house had wide porches, big overhangs, plus a cupola for ventilation. It was the native Florida design ignored by the neo-Moors, and it was so unusual by the time we applied it that only a small number of south Florida architects had a working familiarity with it. Some fishermen thought we were crazy to spurn air-conditioning. We found a knowledgeable advisor in Marion Manley, an architect in her eighties who had come to Miami before electric refrigeration and had not forgotten the value of breezes.

From the platform of this residence, from motorboat trips along the mangrove coastline, from airboat rides into the sawgrass, and from infrequent walking tours along the strands and sloughs of the cypress swamps, we saw many of the birds and animals that development in Miami and elsewhere had displaced, the birds and animals that Carl Fisher could never lure back. We never glimpsed a returning flamingo, but the roseate spoonbill was a common sight, as were the nesting storks, the pelicans, the osprey, the Everglades kite, and the white ibis. At sundown, birds descended to certain mangrove trees, preferring to crowd together like so many oversized and squawking Christmas ornaments. One bush might hold thirty pelicans.

Dolphins surfaced on the Barron River and in all the creeks, bays, and estuaries beyond. Once in a while, a sea cow would float through like a downed weather balloon. Gamefish were plentiful everywhere, and fishing for them was my pastime. It took months to master even small sections of the Ten Thousand Islands, those mangrove outcroppings separated by intricate water passages between our village and the Gulf of Mexico. The outer islands were barrier islands, miniatures of the Miami Beach that Carl Fisher first noticed from his speedboat. Would there have been hotels out here, too, if Collier had not run out of money? Infrequently, we camped on the beaches of these islands, sharing our provisions with raccoons, who used our tent as a trampoline and dragged the flashlights and cooking pots into the bushes.

The seasons of the Everglades, the seasons of south Florida, are measured with the rain gauge more than with the thermometer. It was the dry season when we first drove into Everglades City, rented a boat, camped on an island, and made an instantaneous decision to settle here forever. The dredged ground was hard and solid then, and the wind blew away the bugs. Only after we purchased our lot did the rains begin a three-month pummel, undoing Collier's efforts, turning yards into damp sponges and streets into shallow incubators for insects, toads, and worms. During the wet season, the town reverberated in a deafening rhetoric of crickets and amphibians.

It was then, especially, that we felt surrounded and overwhelmed by water, water on the ground, water in the air that smelled of ozone, water in the clouds that came from nowhere to conquer the sky, then rumbled down each afternoon like the pillars of fallen temples. There was even water in the insects, which seemed to spatter on contact like droplets. There was mildew in every enclosure, wood expanded, doors stuck, bolts oxidized, books puffed up, shoes rotted. In spite of its developer origins, Everglades City in the wet season was what the rest of Florida must have been like before the coming of the plug-pullers.

It was invigorating but exasperating; the greatest exasperation being the mosquitoes. Any letup in the rains brought bug storms, the most violent of which might last for days. During these storms we were as housebound as any Vermonter in January, not snowed under, but buzzed under. The house we first rented before building our own, rented from a deputy sheriff, was less penetrable than the one we constructed. The one we constructed, open to nature's breezes, was also open to the creatures the breezes carried. Soon we knew why the fishermen thought it was crazy to omit air-conditioning; air-conditioning enabled them to shut their windows against the bugs. We caulked and plugged, not to save on energy bills, but to save our skins from welts. At night, we burned coils of insect repellent, once sold at drive-in movies, beside our beds. When forced outside in mid-bug-blizzard, we scurried to the car, slapping our sides and holding our breath so as not to inhale the enemy.

Mosquitoes were periodically disheartening, and we accepted them as a trade-off for seeing the manatee, the roseate spoonbill, the game fish, and the night sky full of stars. Gradually, we noticed mosquitoes less and less, but few of our visiting friends believed we had profited in this trade-off, and the bugs conspired against their understanding by biting them more than they bit us. Some visitors wondered what we had left behind on Miami Beach that possibly could be worse than this. By the number of our guests who sprinted to their cars vowing never to return, we calculated that Nature's Wonder, in this original form, is now intolerable to about 99 percent of the state's inhabitants.

The attitude of the transplanted Floridian towards his new surroundings is curious, especially if he is a Yankee who has come to escape cold weather, as opposed to a Latin who has come to escape a left-wing government. The Yankee is delighted by the warmth, the sunshine, the water; the outdoors is suddenly palatable. What he feels is release, release from the snow, impassable driveways, and icy roads to which his comfort has been annually sacrificed.

He did not move to Florida to bargain with discomfort. He

has already paid nature's price in years and years of antifreeze and fiberglass, and now the payoff is the sunshine state, where the entire function of climate and weather is revised. Instead of a chastening and ennobling taskmaster to which mankind is a slave, the Florida climate is regarded as a service industry, and is expected to gratify mankind. Not that it always does gratify, but the Floridian is accustomed to so many good days that the lack of them becomes a cause for complaint. Sunshine is supposed to be delivered as a bellhop delivers the bags. In St. Petersburg, the afternoon newspaper apologized and gave itself away on days the sun failed to shine, treating a cloudy day as a city-wide utility malfunction.

It is the national perception of Florida as the answer to discomfort that makes it popular only on comfortable terms. A small percentage of today's Floridians would have chosen to live here year-round before there was air-conditioning, even though the Florida summer heat is theoretically no more oppressive than the Northern cold. Mosquitoes, mildew, dry rot, sandspurs, no-seeums, and cockroaches are encountered with horror, and there is much obsession with getting rid of such annoyances among people who put up with greater annoyance back home.

Up North, the flora and fauna are more beloved than the weather; in Florida, it is the opposite. Most Floridians have no affection for cypress bogs or mangrove trees, and in the postcard racks, the alligator is a buffoon, biting the behinds of unwary tourists. In our map of the territory, there is the glorious sun above us and the wonderful beaches in front of us, and the swamps behind us. Our vision is outward, away from the Florida heartland. The Florida interior, and all the attackers it produces, is a source of mystery, and looked on with the same suspicion that once caused it all to be dismissed as swamp and overflowed.

And is there another state where the names of subdivisions so frequently suggest vistas and panoramas that aren't there? No doubt this, too, is a consequence of occupation by outsiders. It is almost as if Florida accommodates the nostalgia in a majority of its residents by selling fall and winter clothes in the department stores as if there were a change of seasons, while its newspapers are careful to emphasize every terrible snowstorm to dissuade people from going back. Billboard advertisements along the Gulf coast might convince the Yankee that he is still up North, or at least that his old and beloved scenery has migrated down here with him. Along one stretch of road north of St. Petersburg, far from Everglades City but close to the dredged habitat of my childhood, a twenty-mile stretch of billboards points to:

> Thousand Oaks, Oak Forest Estates, Briar Hill, Spring Gardens, Royal Highlands, Stonebrook Park, River Hills, The Cedars, Cinnamon Ridge, Springwood Estates, Cloverleaf Farms, The Heather, Lake in the Woods, Heather Sound, Earthly Manor, Timber Pines, Beacon Woods, Briar Woods, Highland Lakes, Ridgewood, Shadowwood Village, Jasmine Hills, Sundance Lakes, Ponderosa, Woodword Village, Bear Creek, Timber Oak, Forest Lake, Brandywine, Deer Park, Radcliffe, Dozen Springs, Colonial Hill, Stonehenge, Garfield Ridge, Cob Acres, Dove Hollow, Country Grove, Fox Chase, Gleneagle, Green Valley Estates, Forest Lawn, North Bay Hills, Country Brooks, Chateau Woods, Magnolia Ridge, Heather Town, Lake Woodlands, Coachman Ridge, Highlands Walk, Jade Oaks.

Ponderosa, briars, highlands, hills, heather, bears, deer, foxes, brandywines, green valleys, ridges, and forests are nowhere to be found, yet they are incorporated into the themes of the subdivisions, while the pine tree, the palmetto bush, the sand, the seagull, the raccoon, the mangrove, and the alligator, the common sights in the Everglades or wherever

Florida is left, are omitted from the place names and the signs.

Shells, birds, animals, and fish of the kind we collected, saw, and caught in Everglades City get their biggest audiences now in paid attractions: alligators in Gatorland, shells in Shell World, fish in Marine World, oranges in Citrus World. Florida's natural springs were never as popular on their own terms as after concrete inspirational sculptures were deep-sixed into them, or after they were garnished with trick skiers and Aqua-lunged mermaids. Caverns in Virginia may have neon lights, and California may have its dolphin shows, but Florida makes Worlds out of everything. Texas does not have an Armadillo World, Pennsylvania has not opened a Groundhog World; attendance at Florida's private displays of common objects and creatures must be proportional to the people's mistrust of the environment from which these things are removed.

The capital for the Florida Worlds is Orlando, which in 1983 attracted almost 8 million visitors, or nearly one out of every four Florida tourists. Orlando is being called the most popular tourist destination on earth, outdrawing Lourdes, the Vatican, the Grand Canyon, the Empire State Building, the Taj Mahal, the Eiffel Tower, the Pyramids, Westminster Abbey, Iguaçu Falls, and the Wailing Wall.

It takes less than four hours to travel from the Everglades, devoid of spectators, where alligators lie in ponds at roadside and birds dive on the sawgrass, to the neighborhood of Sea World, Discovery Island, Shark Encounter, Cap'n Kids World, Undersea Fantasy Show, Gatorland Zoo, Reptile World, Circus World, the Magic Kingdom, Future World, Star's Hall of Fame, Wet N' Wild, Citrus Circus, Medieval Times, Ft. Wilderness, Disney World, Disney World Village, Xanadu Home of the Future, and thirty thousand motel rooms.

A daily share of the 8 million annual visitors to Turnstile Valley is an incredible sight. The entire region has the look of a freeway interchange. The lanes are crowded with cars that would otherwise be assumed to be heading for work, since Orlando does not exhibit any of the regular characteristics of a resort town, but the cars are occupied by children with balloons, by families about to pay money to look at shells, water, sharks, sand, alligators, and citrus, all of which cost nothing to see outdoors. The Worlds are run by big corporations, who either own entire attractions outright or else franchise pavilions, such as the Coca-Cola pavilion at Sea World, or the ATT, Kodak, GM, and Exxon pavilions at Future World in Disney's EPCOT. The tourists seem more dutiful than overjoyed; the whole Orlando migration has the feel of pilgrimage site.

Disney has more Florida hubris than Fisher and all his disciples: twenty-six square miles of industrial wilderness. California was the proper birthplace for Disneyland, the Olympus of our cartoon heroes, but Disney World belongs to Florida. Inside the huge compound of artificial lakes, adulterated jungles, concocted forests, and mechanical beasts, one loses one's sense of place entirely. Over on one side of the compound is a reconstituted Europe, with all the famous landmarks clustered together on the horizon; beyond that the Future World; farther away, the American West; and in between the hotels and convention buildings, where serious business is transacted and visitors are lodged.

Walt Disney himself had the idea of a live-in experimental community at Disney World. So far, there are no permanent citizens, but with all the hotels and ancillary industries cropping up on site, there is no longer any definite sense of entering and leaving the illusion.

In California, where fantasy is cinematic, the movie sets are tourist attractions. Florida has been a dramatic production since before Carl Fisher brought the elephant to Miami Beach, but the goal is to rent rooms and sell real estate on the stage. Disney threatens to lure most of the vacationers away-from everywhere. Turnstile Valley is capturing both the leisure market and the work market—attracting new industry and new residents without the one natural asset that was thought to be the key to Florida's appeal. Orlando is fifty miles from the nearest ocean beach.

History

The idea that at the close of the nineteenth century Florida was still liquefied in primeval stew, populated with less than a half-million residents, awaiting drainage, and parceled out in chunks to an impostor and four railroads, was not expressed in my schoolbooks. Florida was described as very old, its history dating back to the Spaniards. This seemed plausible to a child in St. Petersburg, because the St. Petersburgers themselves were so old. They sat on park benches and in rocking chairs on the porches of the downtown hotels; they feasted on bargain smorgasbord in 99-cents, all-you-can-get cafeterias that put the Jell-O and the lettuce bowls near the patrons and the meat and the shrimp out of their ambulatory range.

St. Petersburg was known as the city of the "newly wed and the nearly dead," although there were fewer of the former than of the latter. Blood pressure machines adorned the entrances to the downtown five-and-tens. Old people died and new old people came to replace them, there was a constancy of old age, not a progression toward it, the sense of eternal agedness was similar to the sense of eternal youth that one gets from a college town. For that reason alone, St. Petersburg was convincingly historic.

At various intersections and in roadside parks, metal historic plaques commemorated the sixteenth-century landings of Hernando de Soto, Pánfilo de Narváez, and Cabeza de Vaca. The plaques told how those overdressed conquistadores had brought their boats into Tampa Bay and slogged ashore in their sheet metal, one hundred years before the Pilgrims arrived at Plymouth Rock. On reading the text of these plaques, and on hearing the inevitable story of how Ponce de León discovered Florida while searching for the Fountain of Youth in 1513, the Florida schoolboy felt proud to inhabit the oldest colony in the nation, which had been in business for four centuries, as opposed to the newer colonies that as yet had not passed the test of time.

But St. Petersburg's historic plaques were a substitute for historic buildings that did not exist. Some of the plaques were anchored in newly solidified landfill where historic buildings could not have existed because there was no dry earth on which to set them. I was introduced to the four-century Spanish heritage while walking on ground that was younger than I, and with neighbors more historic than any building in the region.

The oldest city in Florida is St. Augustine, to which schoolchildren were transported on field trips. What I remembered about St. Augustine was the Spanish fort, the Fountain of Youth where we drank Ponce's cure from plastic cups, the Oldest Wooden Schoolhouse, and the calf with two heads, propped up in a glass case in the Ripley's Believe It or Not Museum. The latter three private attractions made a more lasting impression than the fort, which was government-operated. Ripley offered money to anybody who could prove that even one of his cartoon amazements was fictitious; no reward backed up the claim at the Fountain of Youth down the street, although the exact wording of the claim of the Fountain I did not recall. If you confused the private and public sources in St. Augustine, you could leave the city believing that Ponce de León founded it after bathing in the source of immortality, when in fact St. Augustine was founded by Don Pedro Menéndez and it is probable that Ponce sought gold, not eternal life. The man was a Spaniard, not a Hindu.

Recently I revisited this beautiful city, which has the character of a Savannah or a Charleston, narrow streets, and two-story Greek Revival dwellings with landscaping that is uncertain as to whether it belongs in the subtropics or in the colder zones. St. Augustine is serene and well-suited to riding around in horse-drawn carriages or to meandering on foot, especially down the lane of carefully restored Spanish houses, some of which now serve lunch or sell cookies, paintings, and tasteful mementoes.

At the end of restoration lane is the Oldest Wooden Schoolhouse that I saw on my schoolboy visit and where tickets are now dispensed by an electronic mannequin. This listing and lapstraked gray structure seems out of place in the company of the plaster and stucco facades that have been done over with government support. Across the street from the schoolhouse is the old fort that guards the St. Augustine harbor, and just north of the fort is Ripley's.

Ripley's is one of the few attractions in town that do not purport to be old. Everywhere are advertisements for relics: the Old Protestant Cemetery, the Old Spanish Cemetery, the Old Drug Store, the Oldest Wooden Schoolhouse, the Oldest Store Museum, the Oldest House, the Authentic Old Jail, the Old Sugar Mill, and the Old Spanish Trail. Since St. Augustine has existed for 450 years as a whole, one expects an equal longevity for at least some of the advertised contents, yet nothing visible comes within a century and a half. Nothing from the sixteenth century, when the city was established. Construction on the fort and oldest building now standing in town, Castillo de San Marcos, was begun in 1672, but the fort was not dedicated until 1756. Even granting the fort the earlier date, it is the lone representative of the seventeenth century. Everything else is eighteenth century, or more likely, nineteenth century and more recently constructed than dwellings in New England that are still in use, and not singled out for their age. Plymouth has many seventeenth-century houses; Massachusetts, according to a source from the Plymouth Historical Society, is full of them.

St. Augustine was pillaged once by Sir Francis Drake, later by Captain John Davis, and again was reduced to rubble in 1702. The Oldest House had to go up later than that, nobody is quite sure how much later because all the building records were destroyed. The absence of building records makes all the eighteenth-century age claims of St. Augustine problematic. As one guide told me, "We call it the Oldest House in quotes."

Throughout St. Augustine are allusions to what once had been. A plastic sign in the backyard of the Oldest House informs: "At the time when the Spaniards left the town, all the gardens were well-stocked with fruit trees." There are many "on this site stoods," "sacred acres," and "historic grounds" over which the visitor retraces steps, none more strikingly devoid of material legacy than the Our Lady of La Leche Shrine, the first Spanish mission in America, marked by various posterior objects, a diorama of the founding of St. Augustine, and a 208-foot stainless steel cross.

Historic St. Augustine inadvertently teaches Florida history: 450 years and no proof of occupancy. The Spaniards, who conquered Montezuma in Mexico and Atahualpa in the Andes, who organized great masses of Indians, who left missions and extravagant monuments from California to Lima, exited Florida without a trace. In part their problem was materials: limestone and coquina shell was hard to quarry, and so the Spaniards at first relied on wood and thatch, which rotted or could burn. But there was something more profound in their failure to establish anything of permanence here. Crops often failed because of insects and deluges; this year's dry ground might be next year's puddle. Rich peat in the low-lying territories seemed to vanish when exposed to the air; terrific short-term yields gave way to prolonged anemia. Gold, which is what the Spaniards really wanted, was itself an illusion; the gold the Spaniards saw around the necks of Florida Indians, who they hoped would lead them to the deposits, in fact came from wrecked Spanish ships; it was the Spaniards' own treasure that lured them.

Spaniards lived in the fortress city of St. Augustine and across the drier top of the peninsula to Pensacola, with various priests scattered about the hammocks and barrier islands of the coastlines south to Miami. Nowhere else in their empire were the Europeans so diffident, so tentative, so unrewarded. The whole story of their enterprise can be compressed into a moment on the Gulf coast beach where Father Luis Cancer, convinced that he had gained the Indians' trust, knelt down before them on the sand and was promptly knocked off with conch shells.

Minorcan laborers imported for farms quit their jobs and overthrew their masters. Citizens of St. Augustine were continually subjected to competing forces in their susceptibility to attack from all sides. The intuition of insecurity produced a society in which loyalties were uncertain: the Spanish, the French, the British all had their turns at government, and none could govern. These and other factors contributed to the outlook, shared centuries later by the condo speculators, that nothing Floridian is meant to last.

The Spaniards evacuated en masse after Spain and England swapped Florida for Cuba in 1763; the English were delighted to give Florida back to the Spanish twenty years later; the Spanish were delighted to sell it to the Americans thirty-five years after that. It was, characteristically, Andrew

Jackson's unapproved raids that led to the first calls for statehood.

St. Augustine was a congregation of marauders, turncoats, spies, and profiteers at the time Ralph Waldo Emerson called on Florida's oldest city in 1826; it was hardly more than a shoddy camp then. Florida had fewer inhabitants than at any time since its discovery in 1513. Emerson encountered "lazy desperadoes and land speculators" who carried on the northern practice of putting cellars under houses, even though the cellars filled with water.

A few blocks from the St. Augustine renovation district are Henry Flagler's three grand hotels: the Ponce de Leon and the Alcazar, which he constructed; and the Cordova, which he bought from his competitor Franklin Smith, the man who put up the first Moorish bastion. Flagler's architectural Spanish fantasies overpower the downtown area—one wing of the Ponce de Leon Hotel takes longer to explore than the entire street of little restorations—and they make the remnants of the actual Spaniards seem like huts encircling three castles.

Florida's greatest architecture, its most extravagant expression of wealth and power, is not in churches, mansions, political headquarters, or corporate office buildings, but in hotels. Of all the most insecure caretakers of important world architecture—the shaky regimes and fleeting religions—none is more insecure than the Florida hotel business. Flagler's buildings, equal to certain wonders of the world, were reduced to gigantic and ungainly liabilities much sooner than they deserved. In the 1950s, one was converted into Flagler College; a second is now used for government offices; the other houses an exhibit of hobbies collected by Otto Lightner, founding editor of *Hobbies* magazine.

The Flagler hotels might have been torn down, if they

hadn't been made of thick, poured concrete. And although physically indestructible, they, too, are proof of the fickleness of Florida enterprise. These palaces of marble and Tiffany glass with acres of fountains and follies that would have pleased a Sun King were emptied and abandoned within a half-century as the tourists followed the dredges south, seeking more sunshine, descending with each Florida freeze.

At the other end of town, isolated from the Flagler hotels and from the restoration district, is the Fountain of Youth, from which I once drank the baptismal waters. It continues to offer the elixir, brought up from a well dug in the middle of a diorama and adjacent to a large stone cross. The guide does not swear that this well is Ponce's fountain, only that the well connects to a stream in which Ponce may have bathed on arrival. A newspaper article framed and attached to the wall of the Fountain of Youth entrance quotes the attraction's owner, John Fraser, saying that Ponce "was satisfied he had found something. He never gave up looking for that eternal youth."

Fraser is a friendly and jocular fellow who inherited the Fountain of Youth from his father. He gives some of the tours, which for $3 include a drink from the well, a visit to a small roomful of Indian skeletons, and a fifteen-minute planetarium show during which Fraser or one of his subordinates stands on the prow of a ship and rotates the sky until it looks exactly as it did the night of April 3, 1513, the night Ponce landed.

When Ponce landed is not in dispute, where he landed is a continuing argument around the St. Augustine area. From a spokesman at the historical society, I got the idea that there have been as many Ponce-landed-heres in Florida as there are Crucifixion relics in Italy. I remembered the Fountain of Youth as a tourist trap, but on my revisit I ran into Fraser and his arguments. He walked me around his bayfront, the latitude of which he says correlates with the notations made in Antonio de Herrera's diary of the Ponce de León voyage, published in 1601.

Fraser tells the story of how the coquina cross was unearthed here in the early 1900s by a previous owner of the property, a Dr. Louella Day MacConnell. The cross had fifteen stones in one direction and thirteen in the other (perhaps corresponding to the date 1513?) and at its head was a small silver urn that contained a piece of parchment with a text in Spanish, translated by a Spanish teacher in St. Augustine as follows:

> Be it known by this, that I, Alonzo Soriano, shareholder and resident of Brillar, contributed and certify to the public that I was present at the beginning of the foundation, which is the religion, and is with the rising and setting of the Sun. By order of the Royal Crown of Aragon he made his description at the Fountain which is good and sweet to the taste. It was in the year 1513.

Perhaps it lost something in translation. The authenticity of the cross, the silver urn that has disappeared, the parchment that Fraser says is kept in his safe deposit box downtown are subjects of endless debate. If Fraser is correct, then we were standing on the most important historic site on this coast of North America: the first permanent Spanish colony (Fraser says that Don Pedro Menéndez founded St. Augustine on this spot in 1565, fifty years after Ponce's landing), a thousand-year-old Timucuan Indian town, and the place Ponce came ashore.

My respect for Fraser's point of view grew after he informed me that the last time a reporter dared to describe the Fountain of Youth site as tourist-trap hoakum, in the *Saturday Evening Post* back in the 1940s, the *Post* was sued for libel by Fraser's father and Fraser's father won. It was that article, which Fraser says was based on opinions of the owners of competing historic sites downtown, that produced a feud that is hot to this day. On one side is Fraser, operating what ought to be a national monument (assuming his claims are correct) as a watering hole for a myth. On the other side are his rivals in historic preservation who supervise the government approved reconstructions from a less impressive date. Besides the Fountain of Youth, the Fraser family also runs the Oldest Wooden Schoolhouse, that listing and lapstraked building whose authenticity as a schoolhouse also has been questioned, and which sits triumphantly at the end of the Spanish lane, clashing with the restoration.

The Indians whose pageantry and ritual dances impressed developer Henry Flagler on one of his early visits to St. Augustine had, like Flagler, come from out of state. Florida's indigenous Indians—Timucuans, Calusas, Tequestas—either vanished or migrated with the Spaniards to Cuba. Their place was taken by the Seminoles, often mistaken for indigenous Indians by the recently arrived spectators. "Seminole" is not an ethnic description, it is an adjective that means "renegade." The Seminoles, composed of several branches of the Creek tribes, crossed into Florida in the late eighteenth century to avoid the Carolina Creek wars. The United States government once argued against the Seminoles' claim to Florida land, contending that the Seminoles had no aboriginal roots.

Osceola, the great Florida Indian leader, was a Creek who had migrated south. He fought the federal military until the government tricked him into captivity by raising a white flag of truce, and sent him to prison in South Carolina, where he died. Osceola's head was severed by an attending white physician more barbaric than any Creek, a Dr. Weedon, who supposedly hung the head on his child's bed as some sort of object lesson and then donated it to the New York University medical school. The head, the story goes, was later lost in a fire in Paris. Osceola's body stayed in South Carolina. During election years, Florida politicians have sought to recall the remains of this nominal native son.

Many Seminoles were deported to Oklahoma, some fled to the Everglades and carried on courageous guerrilla warfare in the swamps that seventy years later became Collier property. The Seminoles never formally surrendered. One hears that they avoided defeat because they were familiar with the Everglades, but the Everglades were as strange to them as they were to the United States Army.

In 1980, workmen unearthed a field of bones while excavating a foundation for a Tampa parking garage. The contractors discovered they were digging on the site of the burial ground of Ft. Brooke, a military outpost, refugee camp, and shipping station for thousands of Seminoles to the Far West. Ft. Brooke was established in the mid-1800s, when soldiers were sent to the swamp and overflowed to fight the Indians. These soldiers were among the first handful of residents in the Tampa Bay area. Whatever was left of the fort was blown away in hurricanes, burned in fires, and finally covered in sand; by the turn of the century, it was as if Ft. Brooke had never existed, and downtown Tampa is built right on top of it.

Tampa apologized for disturbing the dead, but it needed the parking spaces. In exchange, the Indians were offered an acre of land east of downtown on Interstate 4, a federal trust acre, free of national, state, or local interference, where they could relocate the bones and honor them as they pleased. The city supposed that the Seminoles would build a museum of Seminole history. Garage construction was halted long enough for the Indians to gather up their ancestors' remains.

I am standing on the federal trust acre at 10 o'clock on a Tuesday night. Osceola's face is printed on the brochure handed out at the door of a large corrugated-metal Quonset hut. "Welcome to Seminole Bingo of Tampa," the brochure says. Hundreds of cars and twenty or thirty tour buses are jammed into the parking lot that surrounds the building. Perhaps a thousand people have collected inside, this is not the Tuesday night museum crowd, it is a bingo crowd, the Seminoles have honored their dead with a bingo parlor and smoke shop, free of the interference of cigarette taxes and the state limit on bingo payoffs. The bingo card has so many different plays it takes fifteen minutes to decipher it: straight, four corners, jackpot, night owl, early bird. On a platform in the rafters, above the haze of 100 cigars and 500 cigarettes sits the caller with the microphone; the numbers he calls are reproduced on TV sets below.

Much of the usual charitable action from the Tampa churches has gone over to the Indians, and a continuous line of cars passes by the window of the smoke shop that sells the tax-free cigarettes. The Seminoles have angered church and state, diverting revenues from each, the state has tried to shut them down, but the Seminoles have excellent lawyers—they always seem to win in court. What a marvelous retribution for the captives at Ft. Brooke. One hundred years later, their deaths avenged in a Seminole tax stamp and gambling attack, mounted on the white man's guilt over their skeletons.

Swashbucklers on galleons, Indians, and now pirates—between the three of them Florida was an academic Never-Never Land. A few miles south of my home in Redington Beach, the suburb of St. Petersburg, was the hopeful community of Treasure Island. Drugstore magazine racks carried excerpts from the diaries of the swashbucklers, with fold-out location maps of the booty. Pirate maps were printed on synthetic parchment, like the tourist copies of the Declaration of Independence. The most famous local pirate was José Gaspar.

Gaspar's activities were well-documented in the shell shop literature. At least once a year, the *Tampa Tribune* featured his exploits. In the mid-1700s, this Spanish naval bureaucrat reportedly stole a ship and commanded the crew to carry him to the Caribbean, where they all could get into the plundering business. Detailed accounts of how he snitched the crown jewels from Charles III and also snitched the king's wife, how he collaborated with Jean Lafitte and Bluebeard, were excerpted from Gaspar's own diary, locked up in some archive in Spain.

The pirate explored the Gulf coast of Florida two hundred years after the vanishing conquistadores, but at least he decided to stay, and that was his big advantage as a local celebrity. He came to our shores after swearing off piracy in middle age and deciding to live off capital, making him the earliest regional retiree. Of all possible retirement homesites, he favored the coastal islands around today's Ft. Myers. One is named Gasparilla, apparently in his honor; a second, Sanibel, was his actual domicile; and a third, Captiva, was his storehouse for women. Gaspar's $30 million treasure, as yet undiscovered, was the object of frequent searches during my St. Petersburg adolescence.

From a boy's point of view, the most interesting thing about Gaspar was his relationship to women. He insisted that women were bad luck and should not be allowed on ships, an opinion that insured his popularity with elementary and even junior high school males. On the other hand, he fell in love with any woman he saw, which for a pirate was a horrible and unpardonable weakness. Women loved him back unreservedly, especially princesses and debutantes. At least he redeemed himself by keeping them penned up on Captiva, and by regularly slitting a pretty throat with his sword.

In mid retirement, Gaspar suffered the consequences of all his misdeeds. The U.S. Coast Guard, embarrassed at having been outsmarted by the pirate during the years of his looting and plundering, disguised a gunboat as a helpless merchant ship and trolled it out in front of Gaspar's Sanibel Island hideout until the pirate could no longer deny himself the pleasure of one last loot. The tale of Gaspar's sad but noble end has been recounted many times; the following version comes from *Piracy in the West Indies and Its Suppression,* a book written in 1923 by Francis B. C. Bradlee:

> At about four in the afternoon, Gaspar and his men dashed through the Boca Grande Pass for the English prize; fast overtaking the fleeing ship, the black flag was hoisted, and his men stood ready with the grappling hooks, but suddenly the English flag floated down and the Stars and Stripes pulled into place; in a moment guns were uncovered on the deck, and Gaspar, realizing that he was in a trap, turned to flee. His boat disabled by the shots from the war vessel and capture staring him in the face, he wrapped a piece of anchor chain around his waist and jumped into the sea. His age at his death was about sixty-five. His crew was hanged at the yardarms with the exception of the cabin boy and the ten men left in charge of the captives, they having escaped to the mainland. . . . The cabin boy was carried to New Orleans where he remained in prison ten years. Lafitte, watching the battle from afar, turned and fled, but the next morning his boat was captured and sunk off the mouth of the Manatee River.

I never searched for Gaspar's treasure, but I marched in the Gasparilla Day Parade held in his honor every year in Tampa. All the regional high school bands entertained at this bacchanal, which attracted thousands of tourists and brought out the residents as well. Local merchants made up as pirates and having had too much to drink invaded the city from old wooden ships parked in the harbor. The invasion signaled the start of several days of glorious merriment.

How much thought we bandmembers gave to the namesake of Gasparilla Day I cannot recall. My parents tell me that they knew the truth about Gaspar all along, but I don't remember that I knew it; at least I was surprised at the results of a recent trip to the University of Florida library, where I researched Disston, Collier, Fisher, and of course the earliest and most famous Gulf coast retiree.

Among the detailed accounts of the oft-quoted Gaspar diary, which in retrospect sound very silly and improbable, there is a file from the Federal Writers' Project, part of that grand collection of American oral history taken down during the Roosevelt administration. In the file is a letter from a woman named Jacintha, who tried to authenticate the pirate for her friend Dr. Carita Doggett Course and learned the following:

> Dear Carita:
>
> I've found your Gasparilla story, all done up brown, with extra trimmings—found it in a book at the Navy Dep't., doesn't vouch for its authenticity, though, and says they don't have a record of a U.S. ship disguised as British. There have been so many requests for information about Gaspar—since 1929 and 1933 when there were three separate requests from New Jersey—that they have a separate file about him, all the answers to the requests saying the same thing—that most of the stories about him seem to be legendary, that they don't have a record of his capture, etc.

A summary of all the refutations of Gaspar's existence is as follows: The Coast Guard still has no record of Gaspar or his capture. There is no evidence of the imprisonment of a cabin boy in New Orleans, and the name "Gasparilla," presumably given to the island by the Gulf coast pirate, appears on Spanish maps that predate his supposed arrival by a hundred or more years.

The primary oral source for Gaspar was the man who claimed to have been the cabin boy: Johnny Gomez. Gomez did exist; he entertained the troops stationed at Tampa's Ft. Brooke in the 1840s by transporting them to the Gulf beaches. If we have lost the earliest Gulf coast retiree to fiction, at least we have discovered the earliest tour director and travel agent in the person of his creator. Gomez specialized in barroom stories, which included but were not limited to his adventures with the pirate. He bragged that he had fought in the American Revolution, which would have made him more than 105 years old at his death.

Absent the elusive pirate's diary, which has never surfaced among the citers of it, the primary written source for Gaspar is a pamphlet, published in 1916 by the Charlotte Harbor and Northern Railroad Company. I note that Francis B. C. Bradlee wrote the account of Gaspar's suicide by anchor chain, with details provided through the "kindness of Robert S. Bradley, of Boston, president of the Charlotte Harbor and Northern RR Co. of Florida." Whether the difference between a "y" and an "e" ending disproves a relationship between the two men I do not know, but I do know that the Charlotte Harbor and Northern Railroad Company bought Gasparilla Island and wanted to stimulate lot sales there. Barron G. Collier, monarch of the Everglades, purchased the Gasparilla Inn resort during the same period; whether that makes him the original Gaspar dupe I cannot ascertain.

From his birth in the mind of Johnny Gomez, Gaspar has survived the facts for seventy years, survived with the help of shell-shop raconteurs, tongue-in-cheek chroniclers, and Gasparilla Day, now so big that Tampa's national identity is based on it, Tampa's professional football team being called the Buccaneers.

Ft. Brooke, which once existed, disappeared under the

Tampa parking lots and is forgotten. Most residents of the Tampa Bay area would never have heard of it. Gaspar, a fictional by-product of the fort, never existed but is remembered, and many take him as authentic local history. Myth as history is not unknown to the world traveler, who in Italy or Greece can still visit the rocks that almost crushed Odysseus' boat, or Agamemnon's house, or the place where Hercules offered to shoulder the world for Atlas, or even the hole that leads down to Hades. Nor is it unknown in U.S. history, Gaspar having something in common with Pecos Bill and Paul Bunyan, although nobody has gone West looking for Bunyan's Babe the Blue Ox or Pecos Bill's snakewhip, much less for those characters' inheritances, while many a treasure hunter has spent unprofitable afternoons on Captiva and Sanibel, probing with metal detectors for Gaspar's chest of eights.

Gaspar better resembles Davy Crockett, in that some of his exploits were plausible, while others were fantastical, and Gaspar and Davy Crockett both died resisting arrest, but then the military has heard of Davy Crockett. Being a product of a publicity department, Gaspar is a nearer relation to the Jolly Green Giant or the Man from Glad, but neither giant nor Glad man, to my knowledge, has been honored in an annual festival in which an entire city dresses up, invades a downtown, and cavorts in their behalf.

The pirate Gaspar is an advertiser's folk hero for Florida folk, 50 percent of them having lived in the state less than two decades, and if they have any interest in the truth of history, it is history elsewhere, back in Cleveland or New York, where they have stored their memorabilia and the old letters and the furniture. Not that Clevelanders or New Yorkers quote Samuel Eliot Morison and spend their free time in the research stacks, but there is continuity of recollection in those places, people who remember events of several decades, with grandparents who remember the several decades before that. Only the odd and outnumbered natives have a past in Florida, and so the past is irrelevant and is invented for the arrivals' amusement; it is the irrelevance of the past on which José Gaspar's immortality as a real swashbuckler rests. That, and the fact that there is no corresponding real history to go with him, because nobody lived here then.

In all his invention, Gaspar was never placed on Treasure Island, that hopeful community a few miles south of my muckspit of Redington Beach where treasure maps were sold in the drugstores. Recently, I learned how Treasure Island got its name. During the post-Pleistocene emergence of the land, that is, in the 1920s, two subdividers, despondent over slack lot sales, filled a metal box with coins, buried it on the beach, unearthed it in a crowd of witnesses, and rang up the newspapers. Gold on the Gulf beaches!

Of the distant or fictitious past in Florida, of Gaspar and the Spaniards and the futile search of Ponce, we knew a great deal. Of recent and actual events that made St. Petersburg what it was, we knew very little. Where did St. Petersburg get its Spanish-stucco architecture, slightly more prevalent than the Cape Cod cottages and Swiss chalets? I would have assumed it was from the Spanish, and not from Flagler, whose hotels were not on the schoolboy tour of the oldest city. How did our St. Petersburg, with its warm weather and its Iberian surfaces, get its Russian name? Answers were available, but one had to research them; our neighbors wouldn't have known, they were Swedes from Minnesota.

The old-timers whose very wrinkled skin certified this region as historic were the newest newcomers, people who would otherwise have remembered the most in fact remembered the least. Every senior citizen in St. Petersburg could have seen it when it was just a mangrove swamp, seen it from the first scooping of the silt, but only a few were here then, the few who knew the recipe for waterfront yoghurt.

Barron G. Collier came to St. Petersburg looking for land before he bought a million acres of the Everglades. Collier got the placard franchise for St. Petersburg buses, but until I saw his name on the placemat in Everglades City in 1973, Collier was a stranger to me. Disston was the name of a grade school and also a suburb of St. Petersburg, but who among us could connect that name to the Philadelphia bon vivant who walked out of Tallahassee with a tenth of the state in his pocket, who owned everything from here to Lake Okeechobee? Henry Plant and Henry Flagler were famous—Plant for bringing the railroad to Tampa and Flagler for stringing his hotels down the east coast. But the Russian railroad engineer who purchased our peninsula out of the Disston tract as a tropical substitute for his beloved tsarist hangout got no notice—ninety-five out of a hundred St. Petersburgers are unaware of his identity.

The city was here as one presumed it had always been, delightfully placid, reassuringly sedate. Not like Mencken's Baltimore, where the making of the metropolis was reenacted in daily bar brawls and wharf feuds, where the spirit of its creation is obvious in every struggle on the street.

St. Petersburg and the Gulf beaches were rewards for struggles elsewhere, becalmed in the security of thousands of residents with social security and stock portfolios who did not have to worry about paying the grocery bills or the rent. Or perhaps it was an orchestrated calm—one of the essentials of afterlife is that the patrons not be disturbed. No doubt it was a fool's sedation; the pirates and treasure of the Gulf coast childhood were chimeras, I couldn't see through them to the real pirates and the real treasure for whom planted doubloons and fictional brigands were only fronts.

Promotions

The Florida teenager of the late 1950s was dragged from childhood by sexual undertow, through the pages of Henry Miller novels and Sears bra ads, through the postcards of bathing beauties and bare-breasted fruit pickers first sighted in the gift shop racks. Carl Fisher, creator of land from the sea, was the earliest developer to publicize his creation with photos of girls on the beach, and so Fisher was the distant and unknown god to whom we paid glandular homage, the postcard erotica having been handed down from the same source as the landfill, the Brazilian shrubs, the Australian trees, the Spanish buildings, the elephants, the pheasants, the singing seals, and the imaginary pirates.

Flora, fauna, literature, and architecture were all part of Florida's continuous advertisement for itself, the advertisement and the product being one. Florida had its orange groves and phosphate pits, cattle ranches and truck farms, manufacturing and scattered light industry, but its biggest businesses were tourism and land sales, especially around the coasts of the southern two-thirds.

St. Petersburg was less place than merchandise, as compared, say, to Detroit, where cars are merchandise and the city is a location. Perhaps it is a trivial distinction, but it affected us as follows. Every year, the nominal natives, that is, those of us who have been around for five years or more, would prepare ourselves for three months of inconvenience (i.e., the bumper-to-bumper traffic on the Treasure Island causeway) by all the promoters and businesses who exhorted us via slogans to be patient and friendly, and who reminded us that our collective and year-round prosperity depended on this one difficult spell.

The unspoken theme was that long lines in restaurants or delays on the causeway were better than industrial pollution as the by-products of an economy, and no doubt that was true. Newcomers and not factories were our pollution, and since most of us had only a tenuous claim on nativity ourselves, our insecurity led us to exaggerate our complaints of tourists to prove to each other that we occupied another social category. One who had spent a summer in St. Petersburg, or who had lived here for at least two seasons, was often quick to point out that it was impossible for a local to get a reservation at a decent restaurant.

Publicly, of course, there was deference to the winter visitors. My father was a teacher, which made us independent of tourism (although later, my mother ran several successful dress shops), and so we were somewhat removed from the need for enforced hospitality. Perhaps that accounts for my iconoclasm. Those among us who owned motels or property for sale did not as freely express whatever independent opinions they may have held about St. Petersburg until after the tourist season. Their praise—and there was much to be praised along our beautiful beachfront—could nonetheless never be disinterested.

Now that so many people in other regions have left the factories to sell each other second homes, hamburgers, and vacation sites; now that the economies of so many regions depend on an appeal to visitors; Florida can be taken as a model for the hail-fellow society.

Public relations can be traced back through Fisher's bathing beauties; back through William Jennings Bryan, paid $100,000 a year to apply his silver tongue to the advantages of Coral Gables lots; back through Sidney Lanier, who described Florida's enchantment to patrons of the railroads. From its first drying-out, Florida was pitched to the nation, pitched in newspapers and in magazines, in essay and photograph and the oratory of roving sales agents. If its pioneers were developers, then its first settlers were the consumers of subdivided property. In its greatest expanse, Florida missed that period of American migration when you could get to know a place before you saw a brochure for it.

Simultaneous with elevation via scoops was this elevation in rhetoric. All the big developers, beginning with Hamilton Disston, did both. Disston, the saw-manufacturing bon vivant awarded the 4 million acres, financed two dredges, but he spent much more money to open twenty land companies and real estate sales offices across America and in England. He was a good marketer but a premature marketer, and because of that, an inadequate marketer. Florida marketing was in its most infantile form, a medium not fully understood by the operators, like the radios given to the Ecuadoran Indians by the Alliance for Progress which at first they beat like drums.

Disston's intent was that Florida be divided into thousands of small farms, he saw it as a tableau of toiling agrarians. It was an understandable mistake, the nation having passed through its small-farm agrarian phase, which south Florida, being underwater, did not experience. Disston's brochures praised Florida's fertile soil and favorable climate for growing things, as if Florida's destiny was to take up where the rest of the country left off. "Any enterprising man, even if his means are limited, can buy a farm, and in a few years, by good management and industry, it will make him independent," said Florida's land commissioner, writing in a Disston pamphlet.

Good management and industry were unrelated to Disston's own Florida success, he having gotten the 4 million acres immediately, on pretense, and for nothing. He sensed the Florida influences that favored the easygoing and the lackadaisical path to success, the sort of stag fishing route that he himself took, but the easygoing path was only a hint in his literature: "It may be mentioned here that all pine lands are favorable for health. The resinous, balsamic odor of leaf and tree, the absence of undergrowth, giving a free circulation of air, the leafy crowns of the soughing pines, give a grateful shade from the rays of the mid-day sun, and combine to fix the settler's residence in a natural park."

That was the 1880s. By 1910, a promoter named Richard Bolles, "ebullient of humor and fond of anecdote," a newspaper said, went into partnership with the state of Florida to dispose of 500,000 swampy acres that once were part of the Disston grant. There is a bit of a progression from Disston to Bolles; the latter is still marketing Florida as farmland, and yet in the Bolles brochures the farming begins to sound more leisurely. No mention here that good management or industry are required for success. Bolles promised "maximum result from a minimum of effort." "A good investment," he said, "beats a lifetime of labor."

Fantastic payoffs were predicted for corn, tomatoes, celery, as if the farm were a slot machine for privileged patrons, who, if they lost money on the crops, could recoup it and more by selling real estate. Bolles sold one city lot, in a town called Progreso, along with each farmstead, so each buyer got both. Anybody who had held onto the city lot would be a millionaire today, because Progreso was near the site of downtown Ft. Lauderdale.

Bolles's farmsteads could not have been worked in any event, because they were completely underwater. Buyers arrived from Chicago, New York, Washington, and Kansas City by the trainload to inspect their tracts, for which they would pay $10 down and $10 a month. The *Queen of the Everglades* paddle steamer took them up the Caloosahatchee River to a hotel in LaBelle, in the middle of the Everglades, where they climbed an observation tower to get a better view. Their faith in Florida was consecrated on this platform; they shut out the messages from their own senses in favor of a salesman's mirage. They saw a big pond. Bolles's spokesman said it was a soon-to-be-Kansas, and so they imagined it drained and tilled, producing the gigantic vegetables with the casino returns. The wariness of all their years up North was discarded on the expectation of leisurely farming, and even though they knew it was underwater, they bought it out, every tract of it.

The state was Bolles's partner. In the continual and intimate relationship between government and developers, begun after Florida nearly bankrupted itself over the swamplands, the state contracted to drain what Bolles had marketed. This sounded better than if Bolles had promised to drain the swampland himself, and the state's good reputation helped the buyers see the Kansas in the Everglades. But government was no more capable a plug-puller in 1910 than some of the pretenders it had earlier rewarded, so the land was not drained, and various Everglades promoters were indicted in Kansas City for swamp-selling. Two former Florida governors went there to testify, not so much to defend the promoters or the defrauded land buyers, but rather to defend Florida from any negative publicity that might deter future land buyers. Ex-governor Albert W. Gilchrist asked the court: "You have floods in Kansas City, don't you?"

Bolles was indicted in a Kansas City court, but for three

years he fought extradition. In 1917, he died before he could be tried. Years after his death, a residual promotionalism can still be detected in Florida's agriculture bulletins, where one expects to find facts and figures about tree blight and pesticides, and instead finds poetic renderings much more compatible with the output of the state's tourism department. One sure sign that the selling of land is more profitable than growing things on it is when agricultural bureaucrats begin to write like poets. In the bulletin of the Florida Department of Agriculture, October 1921, W. A. McRae, the Florida commissioner of that department, introduces the subject of Florida farming as follows:

> When the North is wrapt in snow and ice, the ground frozen rough and jagged, the howling winds sweep across the plains and pour through the crevices of the house with a shivering moan, when stock must be housed and fed to keep them from freezing and clothes of oppressive weight must be worn to keep warm, it is pleasant to dwell where summer-weight clothes suffice and the tepid sea waves invite the pleasant ablution. When food in the North must be bacon, dried and canned fruits and vegetables, it is pleasant to have fresh fruit from the tree. When in the North trees are bare and vegetation has left no trace behind of its presence or intention of return, it is pleasant to recline in a hammock beneath live oak, palm, and pine draped as a bride on nuptial day and drink in the beauties of tropical verdure, while fanned by balmy breezes from the bosom of the Gulf Stream.

Florida real estate was becoming an end in itself. There were farms and orange groves across the north and central regions, there were phosphate mines around Tampa and a turpentine industry near Jacksonville, there were vegetable growers on the dry spots in the Everglades and fishermen everywhere, but the great movement in Florida's prosperity was in the direction of dysfunction.

In the 1920s, there was a Gold Rush on Florida's resort frontiers, but the gold was not in the ground. It was in the pockets of the arrivals. Just as the Spaniards were once lured by their own shipwrecked treasures displayed around the necks of the Indians, hundreds of thousands of Yankees were lured here to extract riches from each other.

Carl Fisher knew where the profits lay; he left the growing of avocadoes to the old Quaker from whom he had acquired his property. By 1915 or so, his Miami Beach was dried out and landscaped for business. Yet at first, even the father of Florida did not fully understand the medium; in his earliest efforts to sell Miami Beach he emphasized the superior roads, the excellent utilities, the conscientious construction, and he couldn't give the place away. A nearby developer with the same predicament hired an auctioneer to hawk real estate as he hawked pots and pans, and the hawker was an immediate success. It was this lesson of the auctioneer that led Fisher to his flamingoes, to his huge thermometer in Times Square to flaunt Florida temperatures, to the bathing beauty photographs that he sent to the New York newspapers, which were the prototypes for the postcards that were the objects of my adolescent affection.

Every boat race, swim meet, bathing suit competition, and party, every bird, animal, tree, bush, and building on Miami Beach was connected to the sales effort; Fisher's elephant, Rosie, was a beast of burden, but her output was measured not in foot-pounds but in column-inches. The elephant hoisted golf clubs for the photographers. "I'm going to get a million dollars of advertising out of that elephant," Fisher wrote. "If we can get the elephant going around the Beach hauling a wagon . . . I imagine that thousands and thousands of postcards will be printed of this elephant."

Fisher's interest in attracting birds with little flotillas of white bread was secondary to his interest in attracting upper class WASPs with his polo field. The only reason Miami Beach had a polo field, and Fisher took up the game, was to entice Averell Harriman and his dignified associates to migrate from Palm Beach down to Fisher's resort. There was a role for the polo ponies, the pheasants, the peacocks; along with a Lord Cromwell and a Marquis de Waterford they were all brought in to simulate noblesse. Even recreation was not an end in itself, not to Fisher, who built his hotels on the least desirable property. Hotels were bivouacs for potential land buyers, a good time was a softening up for a future closing.

Where Florida was a dysfunctional haven and people came to relax and do nothing, certain surreal claims were more important than claims about soil quality or good roads. Florida was advertised as the answer to hard luck, misfortune, sickness, even death. Henry Flagler, in his publicity brochures, had tried to prove statistically that the "gates of death are farther removed here than in any other state." Carl Fisher prohibited cemeteries on Miami Beach, putting the gates of death at least out of sight, the disturbing aspects of daily life were relegated to dark corners, smallpox victims in Miami were sent to the woods until the end of the tourist season, not to protect the public from contracting the disease but to protect the city from bad news; disasters like the 1926 hurricane, which killed 113 people on Miami Beach and left 47,000 homeless in the area, were played down to the amazement of the national Red Cross, which wanted to arouse the public to provide disaster relief, and instead found that Florida would rather suffer quietly than endanger its image as a refuge from the human condition.

The 1920s promotions were so successful they collectively abetted a three-year land-buying riot. All across southern and coastal Florida, across tracts not worth 10 cents an acre forty years earlier, people gathered by the thousands to bid prices upward, until prices reached levels unmatched for fifty years in the future, if ever. Lots on Miami Beach that went for $16,000 in the first part of 1922 were selling for $150,000 five months later; one-acre properties in Miami were priced higher in 1923 than the entire city in 1917.

The faith of buyers now took the land into realms of pure speculative mysticism, a pecuniary mysticism in which value is based entirely on expectation of value. Miami still had mud streets, swampy surroundings, hastily built houses, a couple of Flagler hotels, and the look of a mining camp; once the rumors of fortune were spread to the nation, those rumors were self-fulfilled by the profit-seekers, who slept in tents or two-sided bivouacs and rushed around to obtain deeds and readied themselves to mine the ore in the pockets of the arrivals.

Frederick Lewis Allen describes the scene in *Only Yesterday:*

> Yes, the public bought. By 1925 they were buying anything, anywhere, so long as it was in Florida. One had only to announce a new development, be it honest or fradulent, be it on the Atlantic Ocean or deep in the wasteland of the interior, to set people scrambling for house lots. "Manhattan Estates" was advertised as being "not more than three-fourths of a mile from the prosperous and fast-growing city of Nettie"; there was no such city as Nettie, the name being that of an abandoned turpentine camp, yet people bought. Investigators of the claims made for "Melbourne Gardens" tried to find the place, found themselves driving along a trail "through prairie muck land, with a few trees and small clumps of palmetto" and were hopelessly mired in the mud three miles short of their destination. But still the public bought, here and elsewhere, blindly, trustingly, natives of Florida, visitors to Florida, and good citizens of Ohio and Massachusetts and Wisconsin who had never been near Florida but made out their checks for lots in what they were told was to be "another

Coral Gables" or was "next to the right of way of the new railroad," or was to be a "twenty-million-dollar city." The stories of prodigious profits made in Florida land were sufficient bait.

Florida cities, including St. Petersburg, were crowded with binder boys, sharpies of no apparent means who made instant millions by buying and reselling land contracts. A property might change hands ten, fifteen, twenty times, with each temporary holder gaining a profit, before anybody actually took legal possession. Bloated with ten or fifteen or twenty profits, its value so distended as to be unrecognizable, property continued to be irresistible to a new wave of buyers. Developers like D. P. Davis, lucky enough to have manufactured new land in time for the boom market, sold out in twenty-four hours, wheelbarrows of cash dumped into their offices.

The corollary promise to life without death was wealth without work: buy two pieces of Florida land, build on one, sell the other, and retire on the profits. All of the promoters had encouraged such expectations, and the results were so extreme that they turned Fisher, the most successful stimulator, into a reactionary. He continued to profess the discredited notion that even Florida had an inherent and limited worth, somehow related to price, and that prices should move in modest jumps. He held his property to 10 percent a year increases while people around him were getting twenty-five times that. It was a futile resistance.

Banks around the country began to see their assets lost to Florida when depositors and a sizable amount of national wealth went South. Some states attempted to fight the boom by prohibiting the transport of building materials into Florida, as if a shortage of lumber and mortar could retard this mystical process. In 1925, the boom went bust, and Florida went bust with it.

The child of St. Petersburg remembers a wilderness of scrub pine and palmetto brush at the edge of town. There were rusted fire hydrants, ornate streetlights overgrown with vines, old brick streets half sunk in sandy soil, some railroad tracks, as if the area had been prepared for civilization and then abandoned quickly, as the Maya had abandoned their temples. This was a ruin, not of the Spaniards, but of the earliest developers, about whom I knew so little. Somebody informed me it was a failed subdivision from the boom. What one heard about the boom was that it was unexpected and unrelated to anything, an Orphic delirium that swept across the state, entrancing the people, forcing them to speculate wildly in real estate and to buy swampland, until the delirium suddenly passed and its victims were returned to sobriety and fell into the depression.

Current Events

Collier's Tamiami Trail connects Everglades City to Naples. It is the hump of two-lane asphalt that carried us across the sawgrass plain, the cypress strands, the inundations earlier described, the terrain on both sides of the road navigable by airboats or half-tracks called swamp buggies, and knowable only to the weekend paramilitary, the Indians, the frog giggers, and a few bird-watchers as rare as their subjects. About 15 miles west of the Everglades City turnoff and just beyond the boundary of the Everglades National Park was an impressive Florida-style resort, that perpetual symbol of Florida settlement, an Alhambra rising out of the wetlands on both sides of the highway. It had two restaurants and several tennis courts, enough rooms for a convention, a skeet-shooting range, and a private airport.

Yachts were parked behind the buildings in a culvert that must have led somewhere through the swamps and eventually to the Gulf, but we were inland here, several miles inland, and the yachts had the aspect of humorous clutter, picked up and set down far from where they belonged.

Sometime in the mid-1970s, Susan and I stopped for lunch on the north side of this dislocated extravagance. The restaurant could have been a banquet hall, the latent brightness of its white walls and large windows counteracted by heavy curtains, red carpets, dark paneling. Aluminum reproductions of the weapons of knights were attached to the walls and back-lit, in the tradition of Florida Motel Medieval. Several hundred people could have eaten here; we counted ten or fifteen customers.

Surrounding the restaurant were corridors of guest rooms built around a patio with the swimming pool. In the pool, the filters were filtering, but no swimmers or sunbathers were in sight. It was one of the bug-blizzard days, when you couldn't have held a pose for ten seconds without being pelted with stingers. Mosquitoes must have thought of this pool as their stocked pond for humans.

The resort-on-the-wetlands was called Remuda Ranch. By the condition of the buildings we guessed that it was a decade or so old, putting it not in Collier's era and Fisher's era, but in the era of my Florida adolescence. We wondered what sort of misguided neo-Collier would have invested in it.

Remuda Ranch had changed owners. The original owner, we found out later, was living somewhere in Las Vegas. His name was Leonard Rosen. By the look of things at Remuda, we would have figured Rosen for an eccentric hotelier; actually, he had been in the Florida land business. The Remuda Ranch resort was the centerpiece for an underwater subdivision. Around the hotel/restaurant, out behind the empty swimming pool still filtering and alongside the yachts parked in the culvert, the swamplands were divided into thousands of parcels invisible to the eye. It was too soggy for roads, shrubs, houses, utilities, or fences, but this was a community nonetheless, a community of absentee property holders who collectively had paid millions for one of the last stretches of undredged and impassable Florida inventory.

Swamp-selling from my own time, when I was in St. Petersburg, thinking that the boom was a bygone delirium. Leonard Rosen had worked his way down to the Everglades as I worked my way up through school. With perhaps no more original personal investment than my father put into our little pie-shaped lot on Redington Beach, Rosen became the largest subdivider in the Western world, equaling the feat of his Florida predecessors.

In 1957, Rosen was on vacation in Miami but missed his return flight, rented a car, and drove to Punta Gorda, near Ft. Myers, to spend the night at a well-known health spa. He was from Baltimore and had arthritic feet. Along the road, he saw some interesting signs: "Florida Land. $10 down and $10 a month." It was as if everything in his life had prepared him for the meaning of this.

Rosen understood $10 down and $10 a month because he and his brother Jack sold television sets and refrigerators, on time, to poor people in Baltimore. They were selling in some tough neighborhoods, but Leonard was very tough himself. Physically, he was myopic, short, and bowlegged. He could be ingratiating, but business associates recall that he often wavered between two emotional extremes: catatonia and rage. A colleague from the Florida Land Board remembers that: "When Leonard wasn't pounding on a table, he was asleep."

He also understood marketing; as a teenager he worked the fairs and the boardwalks with the barkers and the pitchmen. He knew how to apply his early experiences to seemingly unrelated situations, so in 1949, when he and his brother already owned three installment appliance stores, the Rosens remembered the boardwalk while contemplating the storeroom of televisions and thought: Why should we just sell TVs when we might be able to sell things *on* TV?

The Rosen marketing technique, an ex-employee contends, was to advertise a product and then invent it—ex post facto—if enough orders were received. They advertised a vitamin supplement and, later, a hair conditioner with lanolin, which they called Charles Antell, with Formula Number Nine. The two stars of the Antell ads were a bushy-haired announcer and a sheep. The announcer explained that sheep make their own lanolin, and then said, "Have you ever seen a bald sheep?" TV station managers of the day thought of the half-hour hair conditioner commercials as educational.

Charles Antell sounded like a French aristocrat who might have owned a sheep farm; Charlie Kasher, who wrote the pitch, had a relative named Antell. Formula Number Nine sounded scientific; it was common lanolin extract, mixed in bathtubs, the ex-employee says, with readily available bulk shampoo. With the upper classes, science, and sheep standing behind this liquid, the Rosen brothers had to construct a factory to supersede the bathtubs and to keep up with the orders, which came in at several million dollars per year. Dedicated to tennis and perturbed by his arthritic feet, Leonard Rosen drove to the health spa in Punta Gorda, saw the signs, and it occurred to him that this Florida real estate was in one way no different than refrigerators and in another way no different than hair conditioner with Formula Number Nine.

Rosen's advisor on real estate matters was Milt Mendelsohn, whose signs these were. Mendelsohn had worked in advertising, first in Chicago, then in Miami Beach. In the 1950s, he started his own little Florida retirement subdivision called Harbor Heights, but his influence on the Florida land business exceeded its modest boundaries. He advised as many of his clients as possible that Florida itself was a more profitable commodity than whatever else they happened to be selling. One of his clients was Nat Ratner of D-Con Roach Powder, who Mendelsohn says wanted to diversify from baseboard poisons to face creams, until Mendelsohn convinced him to forget the face creams and market the cattle ranch, out in the palmetto scrublands north of the Everglades, near the migrant-worker town of Immokalee. Mendelsohn says he advised Ratner to subdivide his ranch and sell it mail order. He called it Lehigh Acres to make up for the absence of hills.

Rosen's sighting of the $10 down and $10 a month signs was as accidental as a rapport between him and Mendelsohn was inevitable. In 1957, they took a ride in a Cessna airplane across the lower Gulf coast. Much of that coastline was elevated, populated, valuable, and yet there was still worthless land contiguous to priceless land—the history of the state as a whole repeated on each separate parcel. Across the Caloosahatchee River from the expensive real estate of Ft. Myers was a potentially superior piece of real estate called Redfish Point, unscooped and obtainable for $150 or less an acre. Mendelsohn liked the location and the price. He suggested a name change from Redfish Point to Cape Coral, to make up for the absence of coral.

Mendelsohn had an idea how Rosen, like his predecessors from the last century, could get the land for nothing. Cape Coral did not have to be purchased out-of-pocket; Rosen could buy a small parcel and take out options on the rest as the orders came in, acquiring this product ex post facto and with the customers' money. Customers would pay more than twenty times retail what Rosen would have to pay wholesale; retail prices for Cape Coral were based on Mendelsohn's divination of what he called "real 'real' worth."

In the case of Cape Coral, "real 'real' worth" figured to be about $4,000 an acre; $2,000 for the standard half-acre homesite, $20 down and $20 a month. The layout for Cape Coral was copied from Mendelsohn's Harbor Heights subdivision, divided into color-coded regions that looked good in the brochures.

The first ads for Cape Coral appeared in national magazines in the spring of 1957. An employee of Rosen's sat in the Ft. Myers post office to pick up an impressive pile of returns, returns from shopkeepers, auto mechanics, teachers, farmers, retailers, tailors, nurses, bureaucrats, sons and daughters of buyers in the boom, plus middle-class and blue-collar investors who could not have afforded Florida in the 1920s. Because of social security and general prosperity in the U.S., Florida was within the economic grasp of every working American. Rosen's easy monthly payments complemented the budgets and career timetables of laborers in middle age, who could watch their Florida homesteads mature right along with their life insurance and their pension plans.

Other land developers who tested the mails got the same results; the Mackle brothers, General Development Corporation, the Ratners. There was this astounding pent-up demand for Florida that nobody had predicted. Beyond the Depression and the World War, millions revived their hopes of escape to Florida and not just for the winters. With air conditioners, people could escape year-round, and end their life on earth in comfort. Many young soldiers were trained on Florida beach resorts, then mostly vacant, during the early 1940s. Now they had graduated on the GI bill, married, raised families, and dreamed of returning to the beaches where they trained.

Rosen hit pay dirt with a most unlikely proposition. Who would send a monthly installment to an unknown company for a half-acre lot on a swampspit soon to be developed, and agree to make several years of payments before he received the deed? Perhaps nobody, if the property had been in Maryland, but this was Florida. Enough people responded so that after Charles Antell sold out to Bab-O (without the Rosen ingenuity, Charles Antell soon went down Bab-O's drain), the Rosen sales force was taken off the scalp and directed at Cape Coral, via the newly formed Gulf American Land Corporation.

Gulf American soon gave up on mail order as inadequate to capture the potential market. Rosen set up his own real estate offices in cities and towns across the country, just as Disston and Bolles had done decades earlier. Professional realtors were too constrained to be of much use here. The Cape Coral force came out of Bibles and encyclopedias, roof coating and perfumes, aluminum siding and stain remover. Door-to-door gypsies, bartenders, unemployed ex-husbands desperate to meet alimony payments were typical recruits, trained by carnies and ex-lanolizers in intensive courses held in states with loose consumer-protection statutes.

I am summarizing the evolution of six or seven years now, when what started with a magazine ad developed into a fleet of airplanes, a printing plant, a room full of WATS-line jockeys, and salesmen everywhere from San Francisco to the Vatican. If you lived in a northern city, you were likely to be invited to a free dinner at which a speaker would give a talk on Florida or where a movie would be shown, and you would end up in this banquet hall, unaware that some of your table-mates were Gulf American employees, and the movie or speech would be an introduction to Cape Coral. After the movie, a large display board would be uncovered, various lots would be put up as available for sale, and a Gulf American employee, still incognito, would jump up and say "Put a hold on Lot Number 239." Another Gulf American employee, also incognito, would be visibly distressed that he had lost out on that one, and in this stock-exchange-like frenzy you could begin to believe that unless you put the hold on Lot 240 you would miss a wonderful opportunity, never suspecting that there was an infinite supply of lots, and so you would jump up and yell "sold."

Out of the parties came the free trips to Florida, via airplane, where if you were willing to put a deposit on a lot at the dinner you would be flown direct to Cape Coral, where the deal would be closed. At the height of its business, Gulf

American was sending out 4 million party invitations a month, through a subsidiary, it owned more than twenty-five airplanes for the flights, a nationwide travel club whose only purpose was to book tourists into Cape Coral, and, if you happened to have been strolling down the waterfront at Miami Beach or outside Buckingham Palace or around the fountains of Rome, somebody would stop you to tell you the Cape Coral story.

Tourists who came to Miami Beach's hotels for a relaxed vacation, unaware of Cape Coral's existence, got invited to free cocktail parties and then to free tours of the Everglades; they were herded onto buses and three or four hours later found themselves at the gates of the mail-order city on the opposite coast. The competition for "units"—which is what the land business called a husband and wife, white, over twenty-one and under sixty-five—was intense. The Rosens, the Mackles, and other subdividers squabbled for the hustling rights to units lodged at all the big Miami Beach resorts. When one land company controlled a hotel, it was called a "location."

In the heyday of Gulf American, the early 1960s, a good percentage of the Miami Beach hospitality was based on the fact that a bellhop could make $40 by delivering a unit to a land company. Units that strolled the Miami Beach lobbies were shadowed by eager helpers and doted upon as if they were dignitaries. Land salesmen in bathing suits roamed the poolsides and walked the oceanfronts, delighted to see everyone. The Miami Serpentarium, the Parrot Jungle, the Pearl Lagoon, an oyster bar, the free weight machines on Collins Avenue, a shell shop, a notions shop, and the free aquarium on Lincoln Road were all at one time used by Gulf American as "land traps," or places where people could be signed up for tours. Gulf American put an elephant on Miami Beach, an elephant just like Carl Fisher's.

Without having learned directly from his predecessors, Rosen intuited and extended their techniques, distilled their motives and intentions. Flagler and Fisher built hotels and golf courses as come-ons for land sales; Rosen built a yacht club, golf course, and then a large motel at Cape Coral. The connection between recreation and real estate was always implied; Rosen institutionalized it. The Cape Coral weekend was free, but the people who were flown or bused in to take advantage of it were housed at a motel in the company of salesmen whose job it was to "wine, dine, and solidify." The payment for the free weekend was the signing of the contract, and in the confusion of whether they were vacationers, guests, investors, or ingrates the populace bought the lots.

Gulf American installed its most persuasive employees at the site; Cape Coral had the electronics of an embassy and the ambiance of a car dealership. Salesmen were aided by secret intercom systems in the rooms, through which they could eavesdrop on the units and learn whether a husband or a wife was resisting the purchase and how best the resistance could be overcome. Through hand signals and verbal codes, "X" and "double X," the employees warned each other of the arrival of certain parties to whom Gulf American preferred not to sell, and who then had as much trouble seeing a contract as the others had in avoiding it. "X" groups, I have been told, included blacks, men with pipes and mustaches, accountants, and lawyers.

Near the 100-unit motel was the largest rose garden in the world, stippled with replicas of famous statues and busts of dignitaries: the Pietà, John Kennedy, the Roosevelts, Mount Rushmore, the flag-raising at Iwo Jima. Porpoises did their routine in an amphitheater-pool. At night, an artificial lake in the middle of the garden would roil up in thirty-foot spurts of colored water, synchronized with martial music that came from the outdoor player organ brought from Germany. Bob

Hope dedicated the Garden of Patriots, and returned in 1966 to receive the patriot-of-the-year award, and the garden was selected by the Freedoms Foundation of Valley Forge to receive a George Washington Honor Medal award for its "history happened here" program. Salesman bragged that it was impossible to wander through the Garden of Patriots without being signed up for an appointment for a Cape Coral tour.

Fifty percent of the sales price of each lot, $1,000 or more in most cases, went to flights, hotel bills, wining, dining, solidifying—50 percent to convince the customer to buy. An auditor would have assumed, from the expenditures and disbursements, that Gulf American was in the travel and restaurant business, or in the advertising business, and yet Cape Coral would not have sold any other way. What Gulf American feared most, more than criminals or taunting journalists, was the independent real estate agent. Only in the context of the promotion did anybody volunteer to pay $4,000 and up for these lots. Outside the promotion, the pent-up demand that sent millions to Florida did not seem to exist. The first time an independent broker opened an office to serve the languid resale market, where lot prices were cut in half or more by owners desperate to sell, he was reviled as a heretic and nearly run out of town. In some Florida subdivisions, developer-owned newspapers rejected as scandalous and unfit to print not only the usual sex devices and phony cancer cures, but also the local real estate classifieds.

What was it the Cape Coral buyers were buying? Beyond the motel, the golf course, the roses, the landscaped sales core, the solidifying sector, was the property, acquired option by option, expanding like the Quaker Oats cereal promotion in which breakfast eaters took possession of the Klondike inch by inch; here it was half-acre by half-acre. Most of Cape Coral was in a coastal wetland, 350 linear miles of ruts were left by the scoops and called canals; lots on both sides of the ruts sold as waterfront property. Depending on what year he arrived, the prospective client would see dredges, ruts, acres and acres of filled tabula rasa, more acres and acres of wetlands yet to be filled, and it might take a half-day search in a jeep for a purchaser to reach his property, if he reached it at all.

Inspecting Cape Coral did not dissuade people from investing in it, they were not buying real estate, they were buying a vision of what it and they would someday become. They looked across the empty landscape and saw their future, twenty years hence, when their Northern work would be completed and they would be released from unappealing predicaments, and Cape Coral likewise would be transformed. Salesmen liked to say that Cape Coral would be the new Miami Beach; didn't Fisher's resort go from this to that in less than twenty years?

Cape Coral was a great success, and Leonard and Jack Rosen became instant Florida royalty, in the tradition of Collier, Disston, and Fisher. Leonard Rosen was honored for his generosity to Israel. Jack later purchased a house on North Bay Road, that Miami Beach address for people who had arrived. Gulf American put up a multistory office building on Biscayne Boulevard in Miami; Leonard installed a private elevator to his top-floor suite. Eventually, he bought *The Washerwoman*, his fifth Renoir.

But Leonard Rosen, who founded Cape Coral as a test mailing, also faced the dilemma of the Man Who Would Be King. "All our lies," he later joked, "would turn out to be true." The tent was too crowded to fold, crowded with believers who expected a city: dredged, filled, macadamed, and, in some sectors, hooked up to central water and sewerage.

Money to sell the dream was paid up front to the salesmen, to the printing companies, to the airline and the motels. Money from land buyers dribbled in at $20 a month; Gulf

American had to borrow millions from banks on the strength of its installment contracts. Even with extraordinary parsimony, in which landfill came from the land itself, the ruts were turned into waterfront, the grass from the lot-mowing program was used as rip rap for the canals, the property owners in outlying areas instructed to dig their own waterwells and install their own septic tanks, Gulf American had a cash flow problem. To get more cash, the company needed more contracts, to get more contracts, it had to market more land.

Two years after the founding of Cape Coral, with the sales force outgaining the dredges and desperate for more inventory, Gulf American moved farther south, into Collier County, approaching the fallow Barron G. Collier empire, approaching the deep Everglades.

Once a boom, always a boom; it had been booming all around us in the late 1950s and into the early 1960s, beyond our sobered-up subdivisions, laid out in the previous madness, were these new subdivisions, new buyers suspending skepticism, salesmen taught the same speeches that William Jennings Bryan gave at the Coral Gables Venetian Pool. In the decade of the 1960s, more new lots were platted in Florida than all the new lots in the rest of the nation combined, at least a million new lots created by Rosen, his imitators and colleagues, sometimes with more improvements and less rhetoric, sometimes the reverse, but then the Rosens offered the most rhetoric and they sold the most lots. Gulf American was the largest land sales company in Florida, and the second largest company of any kind, as measured in gross sales.

For his second big project, Rosen chose Naples, which became the county seat of Collier County after Hurricane Donna blew the seven feet, nine inches of water over Everglades City in 1960. All the soggy records and functionaries from Everglades City were relocated to the fancier Gulf coast resort town, 40 miles to the north and west. The move was inevitable with or without the hurricane, because the Collier heirs dismissed Everglades City as their father's bug-infested lost cause.

Naples had its millionaires and high-echelon Protestants—the green-and-pink people, as we knew them by the color of their blouses, skirts, and slacks. Naples was a richer, calmer, and a more exclusive version of the St. Petersburg Gulf beach towns; its tasteful and functional houses, the Volvos of mansions, were discreetly set back amidst snooty shopping districts with stores that had branches in Paris, the Hamptons, or Palm Beach. Naples survived on AAA-rated bonds, its prominent citizens vacillating between the touring pro, the Rotary lunches, the shoreline, and their medical check-ups.

When Susan and I lived in Everglades City, we drove to Naples each week to buy groceries, marveling at how the fortunes of the two Collier County towns were reversed. We wondered why Barron Collier had chosen Everglades City over Naples for his headquarters in the first place, since Everglades City was stuck back in the mangroves and lacked a beach. The Naples beach was a wonderful beach, supportive of the spirit of the town, the water tepid and placid, the breakers knee-high or smaller, hissing in disciplined cadence across the seashells, putting beachcombers and strollers to sleep. One could relax on this beach, better than along the Atlantic, certainly better than in the Caribbean, where the thought of danger, uncertainty, and the predicament of the residents intrudes on the lull. There is nothing more lulling than sharing the Naples beach with its Republicans on a windless day.

It was in Naples, where we made our weekly grocery trip, sometimes stopping at the beach, sometimes wandering through the Christian charity thrift shops that contained remarkable winter coats, jackets, and slacks donated by the survivors of the Yankee deceased, that the Florida set-up began to make sense to me. I could measure this miniature St. Petersburg—smaller but just as apparently benign—against the fact that on its outskirts were the remnants of a Rosen subdivision, twice as big as Cape Coral, and Naples let him get away with it.

Personally, Rosen could not have been comfortable when he arrived in Naples in 1960 to announce the new planned community that Milt Mendelsohn named Golden Gate (no gate, gold in the pockets of the next arrivals). This was Protestant afterlife; Rosen was Jewish. Naples delighted in its isolation from the high density that had ruined the Florida east coast, and which it perceived as a high density of raucous bagel eaters. If Rosen had tried to buy a mansion in the better Naples neighborhoods, he would have been dissuaded, in those neighborhoods he would have been "X'd." On the other hand, he was able to turn the surrounding two hundred square miles into Gulf American merchandise.

In 1973, you could visit Golden Gate a few miles east of Naples, across an invisible frontier line that divided the placid shoreline settlements from a commercial zone of aluminum transmission shacks, fast food, trucks, and dust, the grit and chaos of Florida's real business, preparing and maintaining condos, apartments, houses, and hotels, servicing the visitors and extracting their ore. In Golden Gate, a few hundred families had moved in around the motel and golf course where the buyers were first solidified, but beyond them were miles of paved and then dirt roads leading to nothing, incongruous street signs, the scars of huge drainage canals, some pineland, some wetland, a gridlock of unoccupied tracts—on paper, the largest single subdivision on earth.

The Rosen land rush was a monopoly, there was one seller

and thousands of delirious buyers, midwestern rubes meeting the city slicker at the inevitable and final intersection between them both: Florida. Golden Gate had been sold in five-acre parcels, more compatible with septic tanks and individual water wells and raw homesteading than the smaller lots at Cape Coral. Gulf American had promised these lot owners that they could act as mini-Rosens and cut their five acres into smaller parcels, keep a piece and sell the rest. Substantial numbers bought the property as an investment, believing that if you hold onto a piece of Florida for long enough, then you can't fail to profit from other people who come later and hope to do the same.

Gulf American, by selling the land this way, had removed itself from some of the responsibility it faced at Cape Coral. If a metropolis ever did evolve out of Golden Gate, it would be via the people's own division. The headaches of Golden Gate would be the residents' headaches—theirs and Collier County's. The county benefited from the tax revenues, but if Golden Gate ever did build out, there would be 400,000 or more new inhabitants, demanding services, collected around the borders of precious Naples like a fallen Gulliver.

It was unthinkable in one respect and unavoidable in another; as Detroit must sell cars, Florida must sell property. One can often find the most important local enterprise by the lack of local rules that govern it; in Florida, even into the mid-1960s, you could go into a county building and take out permits for entire Golden Gates with the ease of renewing a boat tag.

The era of original up for grabs was not so far behind Naples. At Rosen's introduction there were people who had known and worked for Barron G. Collier, monarch of the territory; in fact, the Collier companies still owned the *Naples*

Daily News. Certain key county employees were ex-Collier men, the local historical society was run by an ex-Collier employee whom I later found peculiarly tight-lipped, as if he had some important secrets to protect, as if any investigation of the former developer, who after all was both decent and benevolent, might somehow threaten present-day commerce. With his purchase of big parcels of undesirable land, Rosen also bought the support of the Naples establishment.

The county commissioners also accommodated the Rosen subdivision, even after they learned from the Golden Gate advertisements that they had already approved the "county roads and drainage." These were good ol' Florida boys for the most part, come out of Chokoloskee Island or some other ancient node of predredged high ground, having held out here three generations, since their ancestors moved north from the Keys after the Civil War.

Good ol' Florida boys have no deep affection for the immigrant from Ohio or Michigan, they put up with Yankees as a coal miner puts up with coal—as an unattractive but necessary source of revenue. Their sense of community extended to their own kind: in their Florida caste system of arrivals, good ol' boys are the Brahmins. Rosen was a Yankee whose company may have misled the commissioners once or twice, but they accepted it, certifying belatedly as many Gulf American claims as possible, codifying the promotional slogans into the county zoning. Golden Gate was Yankee against Yankee, whatever happened there was irrelevant to good ol' boy life, and the commissioners lacked the self-confidence and the legislation to intrude. The idea of Golden Gate with 400,000 inhabitants was too bizarre, too outlandish to be taken seriously, and to some it was entertaining to watch thousands of newcomers get talked into buying it.

The Naples merchants with the restaurants, motels, taxis, boat stores, golf courses, and bars between the frontier line and the sedate beaches had no cause to debunk a project that brought busloads and planeloads of tourists into the region. Professional realtors who declined to work for Golden Gate said nothing publicly against it, to do so would have encouraged generalized skepticism about Florida land sales, which were all dependent on hyperbole.

Naples's retired and nonproductive citizens, who had no economic stake in the success or failure of Golden Gate, were insulated from the threat of it by a few miles and by the Florida calendar. These people had fought their civic battles elsewhere and were here to enjoy themselves. They were among the most intelligent and prosperous of residents, and no doubt would have opposed Golden Gate had it been foisted on their real home towns. Few would interrupt their Florida rewards to campaign against a project that did not affect them at present and probably would not affect Naples for ten to fifteen years, or until after most of them would be dead.

There was one dissenter, a retired federal land appraiser named Vince Conboy, who knew the land values and what Gulf American was charging and was outraged at the discrepancy. Conboy gave up his puttering senior citizenship to attack Leonard Rosen from all sides. He tried to get help from realtors, from the post office, the chamber of commerce, the clergy. He volunteered to represent Golden Gate lot buyers who decided to sell early and found no resale market for their property, not outside the sales machine, not at the prices they paid. Conboy says he got little cooperation from anybody. Finally, he wrote and published his own lonely little book, *Billion Dollar Land Fraud;* never, Conboy says, reviewed in the Collier-owned *Naples Daily News.*

I met Vince Conboy the lone dissenter at a real estate office in Naples. Meeting him there may have been a bad idea. I came to be entertained by his stories of the indecency of subdividers and the Naples conspiracy of silence, but I found them less interesting than his offhand remark that lots at the western edge of the Lehigh Acres subdivision, near Ft. Myers, were selling very cheap and would be a terrific buy. I asked Conboy more questions about this terrific buy at Lehigh Acres than about all the stories in his *Billion Dollar Land Fraud.* At the moment of our combined rejection of it, the spirit of Florida had overtaken us both. Stay long enough and resistance is lost, iconoclasts become boosters and investigators invest, this is the inevitability that makes mini-Rosens of us all.

As Golden Gate sold out, Gulf American approached even wetter land. Now, Rosen had his detractors; the newspapers were in pursuit. The *St. Petersburg Times* and the *Miami Herald* had begun to send journalists undercover on land-sales tours at Golden Gate to report on the arm-twisting and the salesmen's sanguine pronouncements, and the general discrepancy between the audio and the visual. In one case, which seemed to illustrate for all time that it had no traditional respect for meets and bounds, Gulf American was charged with lot-switching. After valuable minerals were discovered underneath an already-sold-out section, the company apparently altered the legal descriptions on 1,300 or more lots and relocated them from two to seven miles away. According to state officials, Gulf American quietly repossessed the land that held the minerals, confident that no customer would ever realize that he had been moved.

The Rosens deflected criticism by blaming individual salesmen for ruining the reputation of the rest. "A few bad apples have been closing their deals with a series of Big Lies," Jack Rosen once wrote. "Beauty is truth, truth beauty—that is all ye know on earth and all ye need to know. So said the poet Keats and so say I," the *Herald* quoted Leonard Rosen. Eddie

Pacelli, who directed the procurement of units on Miami Beach, offered a less literate echo: "So absolutely good is truth, truth never hurts the teller."

The state of Florida, protector of the consumer, inherited certain attitudes toward real estate enterprises handed down from the desperate days of the swamp and overflowed. There was a Florida Installment Land Sales Board, established in the 1960s to regulate all the accelerated division that was happening around it, one million new lots in less than a decade. Gulf American, the number one land company, was also first in the number of complaints. Industry advisors to the land board, who made its policies and sat in review, were directors of companies that had learned most of their techniques from Rosen.

Other states, such as Rhode Island, incensed at the Florida laxity, passed laws to protect their own citizens against Florida subdividers. When complaints against Gulf American were increasing in-state, Florida's governor, Haydon Burns, responded by appointing Leonard Rosen to the land board. Now the presumed target for the investigations sat on the investigative body, in demeanor casual, in spirit aristocratic, a Louis XIV in tennis shorts, either sleeping or pounding on the table. After Governor Burns left office, Rosen reciprocated by naming him as a consultant to the board of the Gulf American airline.

What could any land board have done to protect purchasers who back home would spend three weeks investigating a used car, but in Florida immediately would sign installment contracts for lots they could not reach, except perhaps via swamp buggy? Who can regulate dreams? Checking the Gulf American ads, or any land sales ads, for factual errors had all the futility of checking the road maps to Oz.

But in 1967, the omission of a campaign contribution and a change of governor resulted in the land board recommending that Gulf American be punished for earlier indiscretions, especially the lot-switching. The penalty was thirty days of no selling. There was bad publicity in the *Wall Street Journal* and in newspapers across the nation.

During this, its greatest adversity, Gulf American enjoyed its greatest prosperity. The cheapest land that Leonard Rosen could find was out on Route 41, in the middle of Collier's old empire, the edge of the Everglades National Park. Remuda Ranch it was called, Mendelsohn named it that to make up for the absence of a remuda, it was too wet out here for wild horses. Rosen's brother Jack, who had come with him all this way through hair tonics and Cape Coral and Golden Gate, at first skeptical and then a believer in every project, could not countenance Remuda. "Do you realize," he is said to have argued, "that this land is 90 percent under water 90 percent of the time?"

Remuda Ranch, where we stopped to eat lunch on our way to Naples, was Rosen's last and most amazing Florida project. In 1968, it had broken all existing Gulf American records for sales volume. People saw it and they bought it, they got property reports on its watery condition and they bought it; no city lots, no country lots, no roads, no dredging costs, no sewers, no water lines, no utilities—just endless inaccessible acres of Florida mysticism.

In the midst of my upbringing, Leonard Rosen had created Cape Coral, conquered Naples, and finally duplicated the triumph of Richard Bolles, our ancestral swamp seller. Rosen bested Bolles, really, since that earlier developer had to promise a Kansas out there, and Rosen, at Remuda Ranch, had promised nothing.

And in 1969, with uncanny timing, Rosen and partners sold Gulf American to General Acceptance Corporation (GAC), a

New England mortgage outfit. Some say GAC was wined, dined, and solidified into paying millions for Rosen's chain letter; others say it was GAC that ruined a good thing. In any event, just as the Rosen hair conditioner once had gone down Bab-O's drain, the Rosen land company took GAC down the drain, into the biggest corporate bankruptcy in recent memory—thousands of lot holders at the various subdivisions awaiting improvements, several banks holding the debts. Rosen himself was not present to advise, having left Florida to organize an offshore real estate opportunity and later to transfer to Las Vegas. Rosen was charged with having deposited $5 million of his assets in a Bahamas bank and in avoidance of taxes, the *Herald* reported, for which he pleaded no contest and paid a fine.

Milt Mendelsohn, the brains behind all the alliterative sites, started a new subdivision, Rocket City, which resulted in his being charged with fraud in the selling of securities in his company. He spent several months in jail. Eventually, I met Mendelsohn, we had breakfast at Pumpernik's in south Miami. He was past eighty then, wearing a dark suit, fiddling with his false teeth, and still optimistic, proposing that the two of us write a book for installment land buyers who had not recovered their investments. "I know where we can get the mailing lists," Mendelsohn enthused.

Back at Rosen's founding city, Cape Coral, the Florida dream is coming true. More than forty thousand residents have moved in, enough residents to make Cape Coral more populous than the neighboring city of Ft. Myers. Veterans of the fly-and-buy program, brought in for free weekends when the rooms were bugged and the lake water was synchronized, have come back to build homes, plant grass, grow trees on their tabula rasa. The southern end of Cape Coral, around the old solidifying golf course, is a pleasant if baffling array of modest neighborhoods, interspersed with gas stations, taco stores, and appliance outlets. Down here, Cape Coral is a thriving concern. The northern end looks as desolate as it did when the lots first were sold.

Never have I seen so many loyal bumper stickers, either "I Love Cape Coral," or "I Live in Cape Coral and I Love It," on so many cars. At game night over at Rosen's old yacht club, now a community center, elderly and courageous people in advanced stages of physical breakdown play cards and trade reassurances. They are happy to be here. Why shouldn't they be? They measure the Cape Coral predicaments against the winters they left behind. When I mention the financial difficulties of their city—incorporated in self-defense after the bankruptcy of the developer and unable to extend services across the hundred-square-mile limits—they counter with stories of the winds off Lake Michigan. Have I ever felt such winds? Do I know what it is like to start a car every day during 30 winters in Buffalo? These are life's real trials, from which the residents of Cape Coral have been mercifully excused. How could they vilify Gulf American, the company that led them out of the snowdrifts?

It may have taken porpoise shows and patriotic busts to sell them on Cape Coral in the first place, but now that the porpoise pool is drained, the roses plowed under, the garden of patriots torn down, Florida is stripped to its simpler essence, and it is still glorious. Behind every house a canal, at every dock a boat, miles of dredged waterway leading out to the Caloosahatchee River, and above it all the sunshine. Sunshine corrects most defects, forgives all chicanery, makes up for all deficits, excuses all misplanning, enriches all inelegance. For Cape Coral is not elegant, but it is warm, and for that, its residents would trade the best-planned community north of the frost line.

And in the populated sectors, the lots are selling for $40,000, $50,000, as much as $70,000. Heed it well, ye skeptics of the Florida formula: today's sucker may be tomorrow's millionaire. Out on the far reaches of Cape Coral prairie, the land is still cheap, but if you had bought a few lots down by the golf course back in the early fly-and-buy, you could retire on the profits.

Cape Coral residents now think like Floridians, their view of time, space, longevity, and civic responsibility forever altered. There is a pioneer club for the early homesteaders, those who have lived here since the primitive days of 1960. Though services are strained, the people vote down every new tax. The local establishment looks on the thousands of empty lots with fear and mistrust. It is opposed to all the outsiders who might move in and ruin the Cape Coral tradition.

Bob Finkernagel, an ex-Rosen executive who still lives at Cape Coral, showed me round the ex-garden of patriots, the places where famous busts once stood, the places where big-time commercials were shot. "You know," he said, sadly, "you can't make Cape Corals anymore."

Conservation

In the mid-1970s, dredging and subdividing suddenly was stopped. Developers had filled thousands of acres and razed the shorelines with hardly a visit to a bureaucrat, and now suddenly it was illegal to cut down a single mangrove. It might take several permits to fill a backyard. I considered the mangrove that grew up between the planks on my dock at the Barron River. It was no breathtaker, really, more bush than tree. Scientists had proved that the entire Everglades food chain began with the droppings from its leaves, so what was for a century happily removed as a blight was now Florida's sacred growth.

One hundred years of plugging and draining, brought to an unexpected halt. Conservation was a popular cause everywhere in the United States, but in Florida it required a big change of mind. You could get up a large romantic constituency for mountains, rivers, and forests across America, but not for Florida swamps. Florida's traditional source of embarrassment was officially redefined as treasure more by the hydrologists than by the aesthetes. Those wetlands all around us that Florida once tried desperately to give away were being bought back; the federal government extended the boundaries of the national park with the Big Cypress Purchase; the state repossessed a valuable slough called the Fakahatchee Strand from Gulf American, as part of a settlement for the company's various misdeeds.

From Everglades City, we applauded these purchases and the big change of mind, because environmentalism was ammunition with which we could fight the subdividers. Susan and I were outsiders devoted to protecting the town against outside encroachment. The thing we feared most was that some new developer would come in and ruin the ruins that Collier left behind. We didn't know what speculator would brave the bugs, the rubble of misfortune, the visage of the most recent developer failure in town, the Captain's Table resort and restaurant, to try another project here, but we were always on the alert for whoever he might be.

The natives of Everglades and of the neighboring island of Chokoloskee, three or four hundred of them in all, also seemed to be opposed to new developers, even though they once had worked for the Colliers. These were the Florida good ol' boys, and Everglades City was their coastal last stand. Some had worked as security guards up the road at Remuda Ranch, one was a county commissioner during the dredging of Golden Gate, but they didn't want any Rosens here. Everglades City was their town entirely, they repossessed after the Collier pullout to Naples in as complete a populist takeover as if there had been a revolution. Good ol' boys controlled the city hall, the water works, the sewer plant; they outnumbered the nominals by at least three to one. There was a sign in city hall that said: "When you criticize your town, say 'we,' not 'they.' "

There are many similarities between these rural Floridians and their counterparts in the Deep South: the waving at each other from pickup trucks; the gun racks; the beehive hairdos on the women, who are either overweight or emaciated; the teenaged brides; the wizened faces like bota bags; the gospel songs; the Bible-quoting; the drawls; the acceptance of physical discomfort; the beer; the Rebel flags; the use of front lawns as storage for engine parts; the per capita concentration of county sheriffs. There are also differences: the Florida good ol' boys fought on the wrong side or on both sides of the Civil War or hid out in Key West to avoid conscription. Their domain, their medium of expression, was not the backwoods of Junior Johnson. It was the water.

The fishermen spent eight to ten hours out in the Gulf setting and retrieving crab traps. They got up at 4 A.M. and ate breakfast at Momma Dot's, a little café in the corner of one of Collier's abandoned hotels. Momma Dot's was the town Algonquin, with varnished pew booths lined up along baby blue walls and underneath very old and decaying stuffed fish. At the front was a counter, which everybody went behind to get his own coffee, a jukebox with outdated songs, and a pool table, set on such termite-eaten planks that people bounced as they stalked around perusing their shots. Momma Dot was both charming and dictatorial, she served great plate lunches, and scribbled down all the charges on a tiny and, to others, incomprehensible pad.

We had our first discussions with the townspeople here at Momma Dot's and over at city hall. They were polite and somewhat laconic. We presented ourselves as refugees from evil and allies in their struggle to keep out more of our kind. Whether they believed us, I don't know. There was a sign on nearby Chokoloskee Island that said: "Whoa Yankee, Don't Proceed Beyond This Point."

The fishermen believed that the Lord had put creatures on this earth to be skinned and quick-frozen. They railed against every new rule and regulation imposed by the park, even though the park was in a sense their greatest protector from what they feared most: people. They were environmentalists for the purest of reasons, Yankees were what they wanted to avoid. From their point of view, the only good thing about mangrove bushes was that the bushes harbored mosquitoes. Mosquitoes were the regional air defense system against the idiots from up North.

The townspeople joined with us in an environmental challenge to what we all called the "across the river project." The "across the river project" was one of those inevitable development plans that attaches to any piece of unused Florida property. It was a forgotten tract on the opposite side of the Barron River from the existing town, owned by one of our neighbors, who visited Everglades City on weekends. He proposed to put up 350 units, which would have increased the town's housing stock seven times and might have brought it the prosperity it had lacked since the downfall of Collier. He needed a bridge across the river, which required an Army Corps of Engineers permit, which, by the mid-1970s was no longer a rubber-stamp deal.

The hearing was held in the Everglades City high school gym. It was the bug season, and heat demanded that the windows and doors be left open, so the gym filled with mosquitoes, which seemed to be particularly thick around the speaker's podium. We sat on the fold-out bleachers and awaited our turn; fishermen, other townspeople, environmentalists, and the developer's hired experts lined up to speak. The mayor, who I think favored this project and then realized that most of the town opposed it, hid outside the door like a child who had done wrong. The fishermen were eloquent in describing how this development would ruin their side of town. Captain Mervin Nobles got up and thundered about how raising the land over there would flood us out over here. "I ain't no water quality expert," I remember him saying, "but I know a flush toilet when I see one." I had never felt as close to the fishermen as I did that night.

The mosquitoes in the gym seemed to save their best attacks for the environmentalists. The experts had brought slides and charts to prove the subtle importance of mangroves, how delicate a system these mangroves protected; meanwhile, they slapped and flailed to defend themselves against the sorties no doubt launched from that same habitat they said was so imperiled.

The developer's own experts came from an outfit called something like Subtropical EcoSystems. They were living proof that there are new and lucrative Florida careers for people who can talk about detritus and rookeries and estuarine runoff from the point of view that wiping it all out won't hurt anything. It was one expert's word against another, and the future of the townsite seemed to depend on whether microscopic mangrove droppings do or don't enrich the mud that feeds the shrimp that feeds the little fish that feeds the big fish.

I got up to speak. I don't remember how I sounded; I was shaking with the moralistic dt's. Everybody was anxious to hear what Marjory Stoneman Douglas would have to say. It was the first time I had met the grand dame of Florida conservation. I had read her famous book about the Everglades, *River of Grass,* and we had discussed her with the architect who helped design our house. The two women were contemporaries; both had come to Miami about 1915.

Now in her mid-eighties, Mrs. Douglas traveled the state to hearings like this one, in defense of the deer, in defense of the birds, in defense of the Indians, in defense of the panther, in defense of the islands in the St. John's River, in defense of the Kissimmee water flow. She wore a floppy hat that encircled her tiny face like the rings of Saturn and she spoke with schoolmarmish authority.

Mrs. Douglas is a nominal Floridian, raised in New England. She came to Florida to get a divorce, in the days when the southern half was covered with water and Miami was a small town. Her father already had moved down here to edit the Miami newspaper. She goes back to the creators of the land, she knew Carl Fisher, she went to tea parties at the Venetian pool where William Jennings Bryan gave orations to sell his lots. She survived the boom without succumbing to speculation, she wrote magazine articles, children's books, and finally, her epic of the Everglades.

What is most striking about her is that she has not relaxed her convictions, after having lived sixty years in Florida. (Mrs. Douglas does admit to once having written a brochure for a developer.) She has a New England irascibility, she reminds one of a Quaker in her simplicity, she lives in a house in Miami's Coconut Grove with no air-conditioning, walls of books, and a hot plate for a range. Drive through Coconut Grove and all the sham of commercialized ethics, T-shirt shops, poster galleries, cocaine dealers who pretend to be artists, and Mrs. Douglas seems delightfully austere.

Her great-uncle Levi was a Quaker abolitionist who helped slaves cross the Ohio River on the underground railroad. She talks about Uncle Levi, about people of the last century, and events at the turn of this one, with present-day passion and with total recall. When a writer in *Harper's* recently suggested that Harriet Beecher Stowe might have invented some of her runaway slaves, Mrs. Douglas was as furious as if someone had libeled her.

She cares enough about the meaning of words to have left the Episcopal Church, as a young girl, over one line in the catechism. She remembers it as: "Do my duty in that state of life to which it has pleased God to call me." The line, she says, supported the entire English class system, and any church that supported a class system was no church for her. It is that kind of cussedness and attention to detail that helps her fight the developers through all their ploys and stalls.

Behind an uncompromising intelligence is a very big heart.

Her numerous causes are extensions of neighborhood joys and tragedies. She opposed the state's Game and Fresh Water Fish Commission in its plan to put beeper collars around the necks of the few remaining Florida panthers, because she knew from her own pet, Jimmy, that cats in general do not like collars. Against all the rationales of the scientists, her emotional misgivings were prophetic; the collaring program has led to one and perhaps more panther deaths.

Defenders of the Everglades come more from the ranks of the bird lovers and intellectuals than from backpackers and hikers, the terrain is too inhospitable for widespread use, its appeal is more abstract than, say, the appeal of the Pacific Northwest. Many of Florida's great conservationists are older people like Mrs. Douglas who came here early enough to remember what has been lost. In their lifetimes, Florida has changed more than it did in the previous 100,000 years. She and her co-workers are a dedicated and outnumbered lot; conservation goes against the entire history of Fisherizing that made Florida habitable.

In the 1920s, Mrs. Douglas wrote against the killing of birds for plume feathers, but it wasn't until the late 1940s that anyone imagined that the Everglades could be compared to a river, and not until the 1960s did anybody think of the water itself as deserving of protection. When national environmental organizations took up the fight to stop the Everglades jetport in 1968, Mrs. Douglas was one of the few prominent Miamians to whom they could turn for support.

She answered the call, and since then has answered dozens of similar calls; lecturing, writing, and organizing to save the wilderness. She bothered to drive all the way to Everglades City to oppose 350 units out there, and as of this writing, she was ninety-five and had not stopped traveling.

The night of the across-the-river hearing was a rare occasion when Mrs. Douglas and the fishermen were on the same side. It must have been an effective combination, because the bridge permit was turned down.

Everywhere, developers were on the defensive. Up the road at Marco Island there was a hearing on whether the Mackle brothers, contemporaries of the Rosens, could continue to fill their wetlands. Marco was a retirement community with its own nature consultant. The Audubon Society was mollified, during the period of initial dredging, when artificial eagle's nests were installed atop the power poles, as if the eagles would also prefer a Mackle-built habitat. A few of the birds did, and Marco Island called itself a bird sanctuary.

Now the Army Corps of Engineers and various state agencies were threatening the Mackles' right to continue to dredge up lots sold long ago, lots which were supposed to be dried out and ready for building at the time of the owners' retirements. Some conservationists proposed that sections of Marco be reflooded, to restore them to their swampy origins. One local politician who opposed reflooding told the newspaper that Marco should be left as "nature intended it," confusing nature with Frank Mackle. There was a huge meeting at an auditorium just outside of Naples where a handful of bird-watchers were outnumbered by a thousand jeering hardhats, bused in to represent progress.

Being a Florida conservationist is a difficult proposition. If there isn't enough of something, there is probably too much of it. At first, we viewed the Everglades as exotic inundation, then as undredged real estate, and finally as this environmental nursing home, controlled by benevolent human caretakers. Yet how could this environment be controlled? Florida's spectacular fecundity was apparent in our own yard, which during the rains was a swab soaked in frog eggs and mosquito larvae, and when it was drier supported plant growth that could be noticed in a week.

Maleleucas, or punk trees, which spread naturally across the old golf course, shot up to the size of oaks; Cuban laurel or ficus expanded upward and outward, resting their limbs on their own root probes that began as hair and thickened into trunks; Florida holly crawled up and around the creosoted pilings like Corinthian adornments. All had to be cut back regularly; the roots of the Cuban laurel had to be stopped from spreading too far with a large circular pale, dug with a hoe. Cutting back was a theme of outdoor life on Collier's golf course. The only plant that failed to grow was the bamboo, which we bought at a nursery in Naples and stuck in a low spot where it must have drowned.

It was hard to connect the evidence of our immediate surroundings with the fact that so much of the remaining Everglades was endangered. Orchids, bromeliads, and certain species of trees and shrubs depended for their survival on specific and delicate conditions and were wiped out with small changes in temperature or with the increase of salinity in the water table. Birds no longer migrated in great numbers; we could see the depletion from one year to the next. The otter, the manatee, and the snook fish that I spent futile hours trying to catch were all in short supply; the panther, voted by schoolchildren as the state animal, was reduced to a pack of twenty or so, stalked, tranquilized, and issued beeper necklaces by state game officials who flew over in helicopters, mapping its territorial range.

Many of our neighbors did not share our concern for endangered species, extrapolating from the evidence in their yards that everything in Florida always revives, and contributing to the extinction by continuing to deep-freeze a smorgasbord of wildlife.

They were right about the alligator; it had gone from too

few to too many in less than five years. The brunt of jokes in the postcard racks had been endangered in the 1960s after many thousands of its number had been turned into shoes and handbags by good ol' boys already introduced. The alligator's public image, during its down period, was as pathetic as its representation. "One would think to look at an alligator that the creature could take care of himself. A big one can, if people will leave him alone, but there is much concern about his welfare," said the brochure from the Florida Game and Fresh Water Fish Commission.

After the federal government banned the manufacture and sale of alligator products in the early 1970s, the reptile revived in such unexpected quantities that wardens who once spent half their work time pursuing poachers now spent three-quarters of their work time pursuing the animals, dragging them back from the suburbs to the heart of the Everglades, answering thousands of gator complaint calls and consoling owners of devoured poodles. It was then that the alligators' personality was transformed in the literature of his protectors, after all the trouble he was causing them. An updated Game and Fresh Water Fish Commission brochure said: "His awesome countenance and menacing jaws evoke fear and respect from humans . . . unfortunately, there have been a number of tragic alligator attacks on people." This nasty turn made it easier for the state to redefine the alligator as a renewable resource, and to hire retired poachers to go out and kill the beasts in controlled hunts and with the state's blessing.

Flora and fauna in Florida can be divided into four categories. There are the native endangered species loved by all but seen by few; the native common species so rarely mentioned on the subdivision signs and yet glorified in the Worlds and the gift shops; the foreign species imported by landscapers and developers, most of which thrive and are taken for indigenous growth; and the species imported by accident or brought in to counteract other species, and which flourish beyond all expectation until something else is imported to counteract them.

It was national park policy to favor native species, yet in the Everglades (and with the exception of the alligator, the sawgrass, and the mangrove) the proliferating life forms were the interlopers. Enfeebled species were the native species, robust species, like the Maleleuca and the Florida holly, were aliens. The name "Florida holly" only disguised the foreign status of this red-beaded Corinthian crown on our pilings; actually it was the Brazilian pepper, which, according to park sources, advanced itself throughout the national park by smothering its rivals. The Australian pine tree, equally alien, equally dominant, kills all its neighbors through phytotoxic leeching, which poisons the adjacent ground.

The water hyacinth that clogs many of the state's waters made its way to Florida in the luggage of a Jacksonville woman who returned from the Pan American exposition in New Orleans; the plant escaped from her pond into the St. John's River. The hydrilla, a submerged version of hyacinth brought to the state as aquarium foliage in the 1950s, has been called the fastest-growing submerged plant in the world.

The walking catfish was a Southeast Asian tropical exotic confined to hobbyists' tanks until the 1960s, when one of its number appeared on the Johnny Carson show. This and other appearances convinced a Florida dealer to stock the fish and resulted in their walking away from his outdoor bowl, seeking new conquests like a slithering phalanx of Alexander. After the catfish have eaten their way through one lake, they simply get out and head for another.

The Cuban tree frog broke out of shipping crates in Key West and hopped its way up the coast, leaving vigorous settlements, joined by the Bufo toad, toxic to dogs and sighted outside of captivity after a hundred specimens were accidentally released from a cage at the Miami airport. The white cattle egret, now the most visible bird in the state, was carried by trade winds across from Africa and up through South America, reaching these shores sometime in 1942. The nine-banded armadillo walked in from Texas in the 1920s; the African tree snail, which weighs a pound or more and eats beans, cabbage, citrus, whitewash, and paint, causing an estimated $11 million annual damage to crops and no estimate on the walls, traveled from Hawaii in the pocket of an eight-year-old boy, whose mother insisted that he throw it away in the backyard.

Biologists lamented that Cuban immigrant lizards were eating all the native-born chameleons. They would have been less depressed had they been allowed to support the winning side. The remaining Everglades was a lower-order reflection of human life in Miami: winter visitors who quietly nested and made no trouble, native species overwhelmed by uncontrollable infestations of Latin American exotics, against whom the policymakers fought a futile fight in the name of xenophobic naturalism.

Not only were all the prolific growths anathema at large, but sudden outdoor reversals turned sensible policy into folly. As the government began buying up the remaining wetlands, there was a drought in the Everglades. All the sloughs and bogs along Route 41 began to parch. Scientists blamed the jet stream, which dragged the thunderheads elsewhere, but less lofty culprits were also identified—among them Leonard Rosen. After all those years of dredging and draining, the swamps could no longer hold the surface water. Land that the government once gave up for wet, it now bought back for wet, just as it was going dry.

During this recent drought, the Everglades deer multiplied

and then were threatened by brush fires and starvation. The sensible conservationist position was to ask the Army Corps of Engineers to divert more of the water from its canals and culverts back into the Everglades. Two years later, the rains returned in such strength that deer that escaped the brush fires faced death by drowning, and those who had supported reflooding to save the Everglades now had to argue for more draining to save the deer.

That any environment could be balanced is a delusion as old as the pre-Socratics, who postulated divine mechanics. But here in the subtropics, and absent the certainty of winter slowdown, the flora and fauna seemed particularly rebellious.

Planning was the new Florida edict handed down from Tallahassee. The system of walking into courthouses and taking out permits for instant cities was supplanted by a new law that each municipality, each county, each region control its destiny in advance. Four of five of us citizens of Everglades City plotted the future of the town, while the more sensible able-bodied males were offshore making money in their boats. We had to match sewer capacity to houses, houses to water capacity, zoning to density, distinguish business districts from residential districts, count toilets, prepare for expansion. Our contemplation of expansion was halfhearted, especially during bug blizzards. It was hard to imagine growth in a town that contained more people in 1923 than it did in 1976.

The Everglades City Planning Board answered to the Southwest Florida Regional Planning Council, the new brokerage house between nature, the government, and the developers. The regional office was in Ft. Myers, just across the Caloosahatchee River from Cape Coral. It had an excellent staff, directed by Roland Eastwood and later by Wayne Daltrey, capable and bemused men whose mission was sensible growth. The challenge was laid out on a cork board, a multicolored population graph bordered by photographs of vanishing species, and in the midst of it all a picture of an overweight man wearing a Mickey Mouse T-shirt and drinking a beer.

Dredging had been momentarily retarded, but developers were not put out of business. Now they had appointments here at the regional council, where their lawyers and biologists reached agreements with the lawyers and biologists from various public agencies. There were numerous lawsuits. One of the fathers of the sacred mangrove came up here to argue, in his new role as corporate biologist, that while red mangroves should be protected, the black mangroves surrounding his clients' property were useless except as hamlets for mosquitoes and could be uprooted to the benefit of all.

High-rise was the solution. You couldn't make Cape Corals anymore, but you could make condo clusters. Subdivision to condominium was a progression of geometries, first Florida was divided in two dimensions and then in three. By building up instead of out, a developer could save on land costs, which were becoming prohibitive anyway, and at the same time satisfy the environmentalists by leaving a skirt of mangroves around his high-rises. For saving the mangroves, the developer might be awarded with more density, and so one result of protecting the environment was more people per acre than ever before.

Wetlands have been preserved, but the people keep coming, stacked above the terrain as they once were spread across it, draining the aquifers indirectly with all their toilets and faucets. The southwest corner holds 700,000 residents now and the planners expect over a million by the year 2000. Thirty thousand new Floridians arrive with their beds and their sofas, year after year, to this area alone. Construction is more frantic, even, than the pace of the arrivals. It proceeds in gluts and busts, inspired by the expectations of all the mini-Rosens anxious to get in on the next boom.

One can only marvel at the picture of it if all the excess

living space is ever filled. There are 600,000 empty lots left over from the 1960s subdivision boom in this southwest section, and more than one million empty lots statewide. At Cape Coral, at Rotunda, at Marco, and along the new Route 75 you pass several of these distended pre-ghost towns, mile after mile of platted prairie and huge exit signs worthy of the George Washington Bridge. What will happen if everybody moves in? What will happen if the surplus of condos, left over from the three-dimensional Condo Rush of the 1970s, is filled up as well?

The planners expect that Florida will be fully urbanized along both coasts and inland to the cattle ranches by the 21st century. And in the 1950s, some of us wondered if Florida already had urbanized itself into disfavor. What an ignorance of its character and a misreading of its future. The more Florida resembles the Bronx or Cleveland, the more irresistible it becomes.

Opportunity

How absurd that we tried to hide our little bag of marijuana under a bookshelf, when the town was bringing it in around us by the ton. We stayed on Collier's old golf course, working on our house, playing back-to-virtue as we played back-to-the-land, not imagining that half the fishing fleet would go into partnership with the Miami elements that they debunked and that we had come all the way out here to avoid. For all I know, by the time we established ourselves in Everglades City, separated from Gertz by 80 miles of Everglades and by a human barrier of southern fundamentalists, Everglades City was supplying the likes of him.

Everglades City was a religious town. The natives belonged to a fundamentalist sect called Church of God, the women and some of the men attended Sunday services and Wednesday night sing-ins, they frowned on jewelry and disallowed dancing. The major social event, besides the annual seafood festival and high school basketball, was the church supper. Hints that an alliance between some fishermen and drug smugglers would be even theoretically possible were dropped very gradually.

A few months after our arrival in 1973, some of our neighbors invited us to several meals of endangered species, either loggerhead turtle, gator tail, or curlew birds (locally called Chokoloskee chicken), all of which tasted indistinguishable when deep-fried. These people could afford chicken, they were regular shoppers at the supermarkets in Naples, passing by Remuda Ranch as many times as we did. Endangered eating was ritualistic larceny in the spirit of the English serfs who feasted off the king's deer.

The king, in this instance, was the Everglades National Park, established in 1947 after Collier's sons gave most of the area around Everglades City to the government. The fishermen saw the park as an endless source of unnecessary channel buoys, boat registration forms, restrictions on the seafood industry, and drivel about the public trust. The park headquarters and ranger station, built at the south end of town, was despised as a kind of colonial embassy. The more the endangered species list grew, the more the Everglades residents delighted in depleting it at meals.

Once having eaten a few federally protected lunches, we were told that our providers were descended from the plume hunters who shot up the bird rookeries back before the turn of the century, more or less in the Hamilton Disston era. Chokoloskee Island, 3 miles south of what later became Everglades City, was a headquarters for the plume trade, its earliest residents killed thousands of birds so the remains could be stuck in hats. Conservation versus millinery was the legal and ethical conflict of the 1900s, national disgust at the Florida end of the hat business led the Audubon Society to send two agents to investigate the bird killing in 1903, when one of the agents got killed himself.

The father of the women who served us endangered loggerhead turtle was an eighty-year-old patriarch and formerly the preacher at the Chokoloskee Church of God. He was not old enough to have been a plume hunter, but in the 1920s, he had used the same mangrove islands once covered with birds to conceal liquor. The sons of plume hunters were moonshiners and rumrunners, including the old Chokoloskee preacher. The moonshine was made from locally grown sugarcane. The rum came from the Bahamas; it was wrapped in burlap packages called hams and transferred from offshore mother ships to the fishermen's small boats, then brought inland for distribution. Some of it went to guests at Collier's hotels.

The daughter of the ex-rum-running preacher said that if I wanted more contemporary good stories to put in a magazine article, I should talk to Peg Brown, who was not old enough to have been a moonshiner, but whose father had been a moonshiner and whose grandfather had been a plume hunter. Brown used those same coastal islands where the birds were once shot and the liquor was later stashed to hide a third successive felonious merchandise, alligator skins, which Peg Brown himself had separated from thousands of alligators.

Peg Brown was reputed to be an exceptional fishing guide, a sharpshooter, and a man of his word. His colleagues thought of him as a sea-level equivalent of the Deerslayer. He was sixty years old when I met him in 1973, and six decades of natural tanning seemed to have stiffened him up somewhat, so that he moved as if he had a rod for a spine, and his speech sounded as if it had been recorded at seventy-eight and was being played back at sixteen. This economy of movement and expression made him appear confident beyond swagger; nobody wanted to be on his bad side, nobody said a negative thing about him, not even the park rangers he embarrassed with ten thousand alligator skins, his personal tabulation of a twenty-year gross product.

He lived in a little frame house originally built for Collier employees, with a bullet hole in the front window, guns on the wall, the mantelpiece cluttered with pictures of fish and of attractive Costa Rican women, over whom he was in constant negotiation with the American embassy's visa department. Even at his age, Brown required more stimulation than church suppers and Saturday-night high school basketball games, or beer and pool at the Chokoloskee Oyster Bar. He would try for months to get one of the Costa Rican women sent up to Everglades City on a work visa, and if the visa didn't come through, he would give up and fly down there. In return for my help in drafting a new letter to the embassy, he agreed to discuss his alligator poaching, on which the statute of limitations had run out.

We went on a day-long boat ride out the Barron River, across Chokoloskee Bay, around the confusing succession of small islands, covered with the twisted root systems of mangrove trees, the landscape of Miami–Ft. Lauderdale as recently as when Peg Brown was a child. The rivers that separate these islands devolve into subtle little estuaries, and only local fishermen can negotiate the mangrove maze. We headed in and out of bays as wide as the entrance to New York harbor, and at each end the bays would narrow until it looked as if we were about to hit a solid wall of mangrove roots. Brown would approach the wall full-throttle, I would hunch over and close my eyes, and suddenly we were beyond the wall, inside the mangroves, speeding through a tunnel of foliage and with such critical tolerance that a veer of inches would result in a crash.

We lay down in the boat now, flat as we could, the branches of mangroves and oversized spider webs rushing across our field of vision a few inches above our eyes. Brown was steering—I don't know by what guideposts, since he seemed to be staring straight up.

Then the boat would break out of the island and into wide water, and I looked back and saw no opening and understood what it meant, in the Everglades, to be a genius.

Brown used the maze to disorient the park rangers that futilely pursued him. He showed me the entrance to obscure lakes where hundreds of alligators once floated, until he methodically shot them in the head with his rifle, one after another, and then dragged them to an island to be skinned and salted, the rangers alerted to his activities by the buzzards that swarmed overhead. He showed me the stash places where he left the skins, sometimes for weeks, until it was safe to retrieve them in his boat and transport them back to Chokoloskee and then Everglades City, and from there in car trunks north to Tampa or New York. The money he received and could not spend, he buried under a tree in his yard. This supplementary source of income was never cut off by park rangers, but the hide trade ended with a national ban on the sale and manufacture of alligator products.

As Peg Brown took me around the docks for corroboration it seemed that most of the fishermen over forty years old had been involved in that sidelight; even the kindergarten teacher in the Everglades school was the son of an alligator poacher. Brown introduced me to McBeth Johnson, a white-haired gentleman who wore white shoes and double-knit trousers and ran a stone-crab boat. McBeth Johnson was quiet like Brown and walked stiffly like Brown (was the bad back the poacher's black lung?) and like Brown he grew up on a nearby island and came to Everglades City in the populist takeover. Both knew the coastal wilderness, Brown had never gotten a driver's license. They were still competitive about things that mattered, McBeth Johnson's favorite Peg Brown story was that Brown was allergic to underbrush. "Tell about the time I shot a hundred gators without missing one," Johnson said.

Felonious dinners, moonshiners, and poachers—I began to realize that the clandestine opportunism had enlisted the entire regional genealogy, fathers, sons, uncles, and cousins, over a period of seventy-five years, before and during the Collier occupation, before and after the failure of his resort. The progression of illegal chances gave the Florida native a different outlook than if he had simply gone crabbing for three generations. As far removed from big cities as they were, the people of the Everglades were still connected to fashion and to leisure, they existed at the skin and bottle end of entertainment, the raw-material end of café society. Culturally, they were alienated from Florida resort life, classic primitive rebels, resistant to any authority outside the rules of their own clan. Economically, they were in the Florida mainstream, a necessary override of moral stringency, sneaking around the law to provide the lizard-skin shoes, the booze, the feathers, all props for a Florida good time.

The Florida native to whom we had ascribed a noble consistency had no faith in the virtuous long haul, even nature conspired against a reliance on any regular occupation. One assumed by the boats and the daily routine and the skill of the fishermen that they had always been stone crabbing, when in fact stone crabs had been harvested for only ten or fifteen years. Before that, the area was shrimped out, and before that it was clammed out, seafood was depleted one species after another in short-term bonanzas, similar to the bonanzas of plumes, liquor, and hides, similar to the bonanzas in real estate from which Everglades City had been so long detached.

Peg Brown—part-time fishing guide, enterpriser, luftmensch, frequent traveler to Costa Rica—was quieter and cleverer than some of his colleagues. Others seemed to have an obvious eye out for the next big sweep, ready to cash in on a passing species or a passing tourist, waiting for some item to be declared illegal to enhance its profitability. During slack periods like the early 1970s, when the hide trade had been abolished and there was nothing to replace it, the local opportunists could always hope that their prior exploits, for which the statute of limitations had run out, could be made into a movie.

Brown had already been in one movie, *Wind Across the Everglades,* produced by Budd Schulberg and starring Burl Ives, filmed at Everglades City and Chokoloskee Island in the 1950s. *Wind Across the Everglades*—which can still be seen on late-night television—is the story of the Audubon agents protecting the plume birds, the filming of which provided temporary employment to descendants of the plume bird hunters. Brown was an extra, also a guide, also a man who seemed to have access to an infinite supply of alligator hides, used as decoration on the set for the movie which dramatized the senseless slaughter of birds.

One generation beyond the fall of each illegal enterprise, a director seemed to show up here to make a spectacle of it. In the mid-1970s, another movie was shot in Everglades City, this one a low-budget moonshine saga called *Thunder and Lightning.* David Carradine, the star of *Thunder and Lightning,* was well-known locally for his portrayal of a karate expert in a TV Western series. His reputation made him a virtual prisoner at the Rod and Gun Club Hotel. Some of the fishermen wanted to challange him to a fight, hoping to beat up Mr. *Kung Fu.*

This moonshine movie provided temporary employment for the actual descendants of moonshiners who were in some cases the ex-alligator poachers, and one of the seafood companies was transformed into a movie-set storehouse for bootleg booze.

Meanwhile, some of these extras were thinking about where to store a more up-to-date illegal commodity, the smuggling of which will make a good saga for a director who comes here in the year 2000.

Suddenly, Everglades City enjoyed an unprecedented prosperity. The listing wooden cottages left over from the

Collier occupation days were shored up all around us; new porches added; backyard swimming pools dug; elaborate upper decks and cabins appeared on the crab boats; radar installed; weathered seafood companies were updated with walk-in freezers; new storage buildings went up along the Barron River.

A procession of new vans, purchased en masse by some of the fishermen, made its way into town, the sides of the vans were painted with mermaids, sunsets, and mountains. Down at Momma Dot's café, the popular stone-crab look—work shirt, work pants, rubber boots—was modified to allow gold chains and jewelry, the display of which required that the work shirts be unbuttoned to just above the belly. Some men wore several necklaces at a time. They bought them from the gold chain dealer who came to town once a month.

The hardware store located next to Momma Dot's café began to receive more $20 and $100 bills than could easily be changed, many had the musty odor of decomposition, as if they had been deposited underground. Children who earlier had qualified for the poverty-level free school breakfast program began to drive around town in sporty little three-wheeled off-the-road vehicles. Teenagers in the high school on whom the teachers took pity because they could not read and could never elevate themselves beyond the drudgery of crab traps were rumored to be millionaires.

Fishermen on whom the park rangers took similar pity could now best a park ranger's annual salary in one night. Peg Brown's own brother Totch, who lived in a small cottage on Chokoloskee Island, eventually showed up in federal court in Miami to answer an IRS complaint about having falsified his taxable income, and with his gnarled hands, the *Herald* reported, he produced a cashier's check for more than $1 million and offered up a similar amount in property in the hope that it would settle his little debt to the government.

The town's non-native residents were the last to connect

the prosperity to the cause. First we heard that various fishermen had lucked into giant schools of very lucrative pompano, and when some bales of pot were captured offshore by marine patrols, they were thought to be flotsam from the urban marijuana industry.

But then there were monthly discoveries of floating bales; fewer crab boats went out at the usual early hours and more could be heard leaving the dock at night; hardly a conversation took place without some mention of drugs, or jokes about the fish boxes being empty and Miami restaurants running out of stone crabs; and even the densest of inhabitants realized that a majority of the stone-crab fleet had been enlisted in a fourth consecutive illegal trade.

In 1973, we were the town's only suspected drug users, having come from Miami; now we were again in a minority, the minority of non-smugglers. Everglades City for us became doubly ironic, its origins naturally Floridian not because it was unspoiled but because it was dredged; its natives whom we admired for their indifference to the Florida fast buck caught up in the pursuit of it.

Here in the fishing village, marijuana smuggling was called "pot hauling," which gave the strange plant the familiar status of heavy load, making it sound as onerous and boring as crab-trap pulling or rock hauling. It could have been rocks or lettuce or chewing tobacco they were hauling, as long as it brought in $20,000 a night for each worker; marijuana was a commodity first and a substance second. While drugs in California were famous as consumer goods, in Florida they became famous as export-import items.

The youth of Everglades City, protected against such evil influences by their families and by their church, learned about marijuana the way children of industrial England learned about coal, collecting forgotten bits of it from the river banks, from the truck beds, from the ground. Eventually, they smoked it; some of the smugglers did not like this result, others concluded that pot was not half as bad as liquor. Some bought celebratory cocaine or Quaaludes; marijuana smoking might not lead to heavier drugs, but marijuana profits did, and by 1979, it was not unusual to see fishermen with runny coke noses.

Everglades City's burgeoning new trade was left largely undisturbed by the local law, because in several families the uncle was a policeman and the cousin the pot hauler, or the father the policeman and the mother the town librarian and the son the pot hauler, or even the son the policeman and the father the pot hauler. Garold Glendening of the Florida Marine Patrol, a state law-enforcement agency, was sent to Everglades City in part to put a stop to this. Glendening bought a house right next to the one we had just constructed; for months we watched him try to catch a smuggler. I used to feel sorry for Glendening, having to take his patrol boat out on mosquito-infested nights, when the entire town knew it the instant he stepped onto the dock.

On the other side of Glendening was Richard Wolferts, a local fisherman and one of the first to be arrested, not in Everglades City but somewhere up the coast. The night before he went to jail, Wolferts gave a huge party, attended by more than half the town, including all the local deputies and a majority of the local smugglers. He dressed up in a black-and-white convict suit and seemed to be in great humor, on the wall near the serving line for the barbecued wild hog he put up a wooden plaque, the kind used in mounting stuffed fish, but his prized catch was a burlap bale. Deputies and smugglers danced and reveled for hours in suspicious togetherness. Glendening was on the night shift, he had to leave the party and all his targets to go out on futile patrol.

Glendening's hard work paid off the night of March 27, 1978, when he arrested McBeth Johnson, run aground on an oyster bar off Chokoloskee Island, his props still churning and his crab boat full of marijuana. Johnson was the town elder with the bad back, Peg Brown's old poaching companion.

If anyone still believed that marijuana smuggling was a young man's enterprise, the McBeth Johnson arrest disproved it. Johnson was a personal link between alligators and drugs, part of the plume-liquor-alligator-marijuana continuum, going back seventy-five years to the area's earliest inhabitants.

I sat at home and in my office at city hall contemplating all this as my friends and I put the finishing touches on the plan for orderly growth and development.

In other towns north of Everglades City and south to the Keys they hauled pot without reservation until fishermen were thankful not for seafood but for Colombia, their enemy was not bad weather but a bust, their measure of the passage of time was no longer the fattening of the mullet or the opening of the crab season but the arrival of a mother ship. Local sheriffs elected on drug clean-up platforms and then paid thousands of dollars a night to let the shipments through had to dissemble to some extent—occasionally they posed triumphantly for the newspapers alongside some marijuana plant seized in a backyard, or alongside some Baggie confiscated from a high school student.

There were so many drugs everywhere in Florida that confiscations were distinguished with brand names like Operation Sunburn, Operation Grouper, Black Tuna—the names of busts, for some reason, more indigenous-sounding than the names of subdivisions. Some economic reckoners said that smuggling, not tourism, was the biggest state industry. Certainly, it was the biggest industry in Everglades City and doubtless in Miami as well. In the Miami area, marijuana literally fell out of the skies.

A bale of it broke through the roof of a house and nearly killed a man. Bales were so prevalent that police lobbied for a change in the rules of evidence because they lacked storage space to keep the bales until the trials. Florida Power and Light burned marijuana in the generators—736 pounds of marijuana equals one barrel of oil was the new Florida-inspired energy calculation.

Perhaps any state, any region, any culture would not have resisted this profitable opportunity. Yet I was astonished by the universality of it, by the tacit support of the local establishment, without which a felony could never have become the state's major source of revenue. Is there in the Florida setting, I wondered, a peculiar penchant for crime that exists around the carnival of its real estate and beyond the purview of millions of its J. Edgar Hoover-loving retirees?

Florida's current attorney general, Jim Smith, told a congressional committee that "Through an accident of nature and geography, Florida has become an international port of entry for most of the illicit drugs entering the United States." The "accident of geography" speech is standard with politicians and state officials who must explain to Rotary clubs and chambers of commerce how marijuana came to be Florida's biggest industry. The officials do not stop at saying that smuggling is a *result* of geography. That in itself would be enough to divert the blame from society to the coastline full of hiding places, or to the latitudes, which stick the state like a nose into the sewers of the Caribbean. They always are careful to add that the geography itself is an "accident," thus diverting the blame from whatever gods laid out the continent.

What sort of accident is this? One that repeats itself, certainly; the last time so many officials blamed a crime on geography was during Prohibition. Florida had more nature in which to disappear back then. How similar the modus operandi for both drugs and liquor: right down to the wrapping of the product in burlap (the marijuana package called square grouper; the liquor package, a ham), the transporting of it over the same sea routes, the cutting of it with some cheaper substance (with booze, it was water; with cocaine, laxatives, Drano, or powdered milk), the manufacture of high-speed boats to outrun the Coast Guard (in the 1970s, cigarette skiffs that claw the water like sequined fingernails; in the 1920s, it was Nuta-built thirty-four-footers with twin Liberty engines), the endless confiscation of these boats, stacked like attic trophies along the Miami River, the frequent murders (the per capita rate higher in 1925 than in 1981, we were recently relieved to discover, in a report entitled "Historic Trends in Dade County Homicides"), the proud list of seizures (government announces $1 million in liquor seized in 1926–28, sheriff's department closes down 300 stills in the Everglades, recalls 1,820 gallons of moonshine, 3,640 quarts of liquor, 72,500 gallons of mash, 25,352 bottles of home brew, federal agents pour 240 bottles and 25 gallons of moonshine down a Miami manhole, in the presence of amazed and unhappy onlookers).

It is 1922 and Colonel L. C. Nutt of the federal special smuggling task force is leading an interagency squadron of naval aircraft, sub chasers, Coast Guard patrol boats, undercover investigators, and prosecutors into Miami. The feds have picked Florida for concentrated attack because Florida is called the "leakiest spot in the nation" by numerous observers, among them N.Y. Congressman Fiorello LaGuardia; the *New York Times* says that drinking here is "safer in Florida than anywhere else in these dry states"; and the *Miami Herald* editorializes that "clandestine traffic in illicit liquor has grown to such proportions in the city and county that it reveals a revolting state of affairs."

Florida was born in temperance, that is the irony of it: less than a decade before it got so leaky here, various Florida subdivisions had adopted their own voluntary prohibition ordinances. Miami's developer-founder, Henry Flagler, wanted to start the city piously from scratch. Anti-liquor clauses were written into the first deeds; anybody who used his property for selling or distributing intoxicants would lose the land to the previous owner. Over on Miami Beach, Carl Fisher (who later pickled his liver) did not oppose liquor altogther, but he disliked uninhibited carousing. He founded Miami Beach as a gentlemen's preserve for vigorous and healthy outdoor sports.

From extraordinary temperance to extraordinary leakiness, it is the coexistence of extremes that still makes Florida seem at once like a neighborhood Tupperware party and folly of felons, a Mickey Mouse Club and a celebration of mobsters, a superego of moralists struggling against the good time that Florida advertised. Good times needed liquor, liquor was consecration of the belief that paradise should be naughty, and so little booze joints sprang up outside the boundaries of the locally legislated sobriety.

National Prohibition was imposed at the beginning of the Florida boom. Miami was a mud town and less than ten years connected it to the nation via Flagler's train. With no industry to which the virtues of pluck and luck applied, the model for economics was real estate, and land had gone from $10 an acre to $10,000 an acre in a matter of months. The only substance besides land that offered a similar return was illegal liquor, which first sold for less than $10 a quart and then rose to more than $100 a quart, diluted. The quick fortunes of the binder boys were eclipsed by the quick fortunes of rumrunners, people like Bill McCoy (the "real McCoy," who didn't cut his product), Cleo and Bootleg Sue, Havana Kitty and Jiggy Donahue, Stingray Jake Bunton.

Federal authorities estimated that Prohibition was 75 percent less enforceable in Florida than in other states, and not because of its natural hiding places. Like some of their successors in the marijuana trade, the rumrunners didn't have to hide anything. Policemen, bankers, judges, lawyers were all tied up in the business in Miami, where there was no corresponding legitimate industry to support bribes and boodle. The brother of the prosecuting attorney of Dade County—Miami's county—was arrested with a boatload. As soon as six bootleg policemen were removed from office, their replacements were implicated in the same business. Rumrunners were the toast of the clubs; they bought the biggest houses. Along with the real estate speculators, they were Miami's first aristocracy.

Tourists demanded tolerance, and so the rewards of tolerance outweighed the demands of conviction. In its editorial section, the *Miami Herald* opposed the bootleggers, the violence, the illegal trade; but then every time the police collared a suspect who was also a tourist, the newspaper blasted the police on the front page. Searches and seizures of any Miami visitor were by definition unreasonable. The mistaken arrest of a delegate to a 1920 dental convention (even then, they had dental conventions) brought out a banner headline: "Officers Carry Out Enforcement of Prohi Amendment in High-Handed and Autocratic Manner." The *Herald* pointed out that the dentist invested heavily in Miami real estate on previous visits and wondered how "this might affect the tourist trade next winter."

The *Herald* worried, contradictorily, if Miami's national reputation for legal laxity would keep away the visitors. In a boosters' denial, newspaper executives and politicians criticized the "imaginative" stories published in out-of-town magazines by journalists who had come to Miami and described the obvious, nothing more fanciful than what the *Herald* itself had written.*

An overwhelming Florida spirit of rebellion exceeded

* Much of the information for this chapter is taken from "Miami's Bootleg Boom: A Decade of Prohibition," a master's thesis submitted to the University of Miami by Patricia Buchanan in January, 1967.

all calculations of profit or loss, exceeded the limits of self-interest. Was it the location—the distance from national authority, the low-lying geology, the nose in the Caribbean, the climate, the water that promises escape on all sides, or the influence of so many consciences on vacation—that made the Coast Guard, and not the smugglers, into local Public Enemy Number One? Red Shannon was a Miami rumrunner and supplier of local hotels; finally the Coast Guard caught up to him and his Liberty engines and chased him around Biscayne Bay. Shots were fired, Shannon was killed, the guests of Carl Fisher's Flamingo Hotel could see it all from the hotel dock. Four Coast Guardsmen were indicted by a local Miami judge for manslaughter, and then, after the Coast Guard refused to accept the subpoenas, the state of Florida filed murder charges against them. The case was diplomatically postponed and the men were exonerated, but Miami had chosen its side.

This was the town that Colonel L. C. Nutt promised to rescue via his federal task force in 1922. His entry was triumphal; the colonel was amazed at the ease of gathering the incriminating facts. "Col. Nutt's Forces Unearth Sensational Evidence," the *Herald* said. "Banks Involved in Booze Trade," another headline informed. And after several weeks of sleuthing, forty federal agents in eight squads struck in a surprise attack on March 20. They raided Jack's Chili Parlor, a speakeasy called the Hillcrest just off Dixie Highway, and a fish house near the South Miami Bridge.

Miami had been tipped off. The real surprise was that the Nutt forces nabbed anybody; they only managed to arrest 20 people. "Prohi Raids Prove Failure," the *Herald* headline said. Those arrested were not overly concerned even then—the entire federal effort on land, sea, and air resulted in six convictions. The *New York Times* reported that Col. Nutt retreated from Miami: "before he was laughed out of the state, but not before the snickers were audible."

In 1982, Vice President George Bush brought his federal

task force to Miami: airplanes, undercover agents, support on ground, sea, and air, united to stop the drug traffic. "Halt Flow of Drug Money, State Urged," the *Herald* headline said. There are spectacular busts all over south Florida, more arrests in the Customs lines, the feds are amazed at the ease of getting evidence. Bush claims victory in the paper, but then a few months later, one opens the *Herald* to find a front-page article on the cocaine glut. So much cocaine has found its way to Miami that the price has collapsed.

The Bush task force may be discouraged but it is not disbanded; the only difference between Bush and the colonel is that nobody laughs in public anymore.

Soon the populist phase ended and the neighborhood bootleggers and local rumrunners gave way to out-of-state interests. Prohibition brought organized crime to Florida. If we follow organized crime back to its first Florida appearance, as we have traced the land itself back to its first dredgers, we end up at the same spot. Miami Beach, the founding muckspit, was also the home of Florida's founding Mafioso, Al Capone.

Perhaps Capone's arrival can be blamed on the accident of geography. He told the newspapers that geography is what attracted him to the Miami area. He was talking about Carl Fisher's Venetian canals, which he said reminded him of Italy, the "sunny Italy of the New World." But Capone had sought residence in at least ten other cities from Kansas to Georgia and none had made him feel comfortable. The Miami area offered Capone something far more gratifying than the scenery of Italy: acceptance.

It was not total acceptance, because the Miami newspapers berated this visitor as newspapers everywhere had done. But beyond the superficial outrage at his presence here, Capone was treated with unusual hospitality. He enjoyed the tolerance of hoteliers with empty suites, and of real estate agents with no immediate prospects. When he arrived in 1927, Florida was in its bust market, and any potential land buyer looked good.

So in his role as mayor of Miami Beach, J. N. Lummus, Jr., going through the motions that the mayors of other cities had already ritualized, announced that Capone was "unwelcome." Mayor Lummus said that he had told the gangster as much to his face. But in his role as realtor (what else would he have been?) Lummus secretly searched for a nice house for Capone and finally found one, over on a satellite island dredged up by Carl Fisher.

The symbiosis between Florida crime and Florida real estate is internalized in the person of Lummus, who as a citizen rejected Capone but as a businessman could not afford to. The mayor was criticized when his private dealings with the gangster were exposed, but he was not removed from office; too many in his constituency would have done the same. Binder boys were gone, people were broke, tourists were scared off by the 1926 hurricane. As war can rescue the national economy, it was organized crime that rescued south Florida, via sizable property transfers between the likes of Carl Fisher and his clients, to the likes of Capone, Tony Accardo, and Frank Nitti.

The Fisher-lured Miami Beach regulars, whose fortunes were made on yeast or automobile parts and who swam, played polo, and raced boats, gave way to Capone-lured arrivistes, who got rich on liquor, prostitution, and gambling and took the Miami Beach action indoors. Fisher, who despised casinos, sold one of his own houses, left on a trip, and returned to find a roulette wheel had been installed in the bedroom. That kind of change was typical in the Capone phase, the second and more abstracted level in the beach's development, when flamingoes, elephants, and singing seals were no longer necessary, and tourists left their rooms only to lay at poolside, get a manicure and tan, and conserve energy for later carousing.

Fisher himself resisted Capone as he had resisted the binder boys during the boom. He figured that Capone would ruin more Miami Beach business than he and his followers transacted, and also that Capone would forever alienate the Palm Beach crowd from Fisher's polo ponies: who wanted to play chukkers with Scarface? The developer masterminded a judicial hearing to oust the gangster as a threat to public safety, but his effort was futile. Capone got a favorable ruling at the hearing, and he was the last gangster that anybody of importance on Miami Beach ever tried to expel.

Gangsters were attracted to Florida for the same reason the captains of legalized industry were. They were warm-weather seekers, treating themselves to the sunny spoils in a place that had no memory of what it was they had actually done. Florida, for them, was an afterlife with no final judgment, not so much for Capone, who got continuous front-page publicity, but for some of the others, who could rest here beyond the reach of their critics and enemies, an advantage later lost with jet airplanes.

Like the temperate developers who preceded them, Capone, Nitti, et al. were too energetic to retire. They bought hotels, they bought nightclubs; the Cleveland syndicate teamed up to rebuild part of Coral Gables. There was a period in the 1940s when each city's mob ran its Miami resort: the Frank Erickson people from New York had the Wofford; Philly was headquartered at the Sands; the Detroit Purple Gang occupied the Grand. Joe Massei reportedly ran the Detroit Lottery from the telephone outside a Miami Beach barber shop; a Chicago punchboard king invested in the Saxony.

This open and bloodless competition among mobs was unusual, but Florida was as much an escape for them as it was for everybody else. Mafia bosses, here liberated from the restraints of their northern etiquette, designated Miami a special and permissive zone where normal rules of the underworld did not apply.

The migrating illegals also took over local illegal gambling concessions, which could be found in the lobbies or cabanas of hotels, or in special rooms of the nightclubs. In another case of moral overlay conflicting with the demands of recreation, Florida could neither admit that it allowed casinos, nor allow them to be abolished. This conflict resulted in a compromise where casinos were seen everywhere in fact, but were invisible in theory. One illegal Florida casino remained open for more than fifty years.

The contributions of the new out-of-town management to the Miami Beach casino-nightclub business included crooked wheels, an increase in the protection budget, the importation of professional entertainers who had nothing to do with the mob (Joe. E. Lewis, George Jessel, Al Jolson, Eddie Cantor, Sophie Tucker, Helen Morgan) and the importation of professional bouncers (Jake Guzik, Nitti, Accardo).

An envy at the profits from gambling and a general lack of funds resulting from its reluctance to levy taxes led Florida's government into an alliance with criminals that is as unseemly as its alliance with swamp sellers. In 1931, Florida legalized pari-mutuel wagering. The state shared revenues at Tropical Park Racetrack, first with the Canadian bootleg interests who invested in it and managed it; and later with friends and associates of Meyer Lansky and Al Capone, who bought it through various fronts.

We can get an idea of how completely the Capone faction dominated the political and economic life of the Miami area from a report that Carl Fisher's detective, still shadowing the gangster, sent to the developer in December, 1930:

> In my last letter I told you I would try to find out how Capone was operating on the Beach, and who was taking care of

him. The Island Club opened this past winter, January 15th, under a new management, and Capone has one-fourth interest for which he paid $25,000 to the present owners. He also had a one-fourth interest in the Floridian Hotel gambling room, in which he installed crooked gambling devices. He had two Chicago gun men stationed in this room at $40 a night to protect it from any outside interference. He also owns the controlling interest in the South Beach dog track, and Carter's gambling house, as well as Albert Bouche's Villa Venice. He tried to muscle in at the Deauville Casino, but was refused, and after some kind of a threat, some men were brought from New York to protect the Deauville from Capone's crowd.

The pay-off for gambling on the beach this winter was as follows: Dan Chappel, our recently elected representative from this district, was the collector from the Sheriff's office under the guise of attorney for his clients, and any gambling house opening in Miami Beach had to have the OK of our city manager Renshaw. . . . Renshaw and other councilmen were the ones who seemed to have control of these privileges from the City's standpoint.

A casino was raided one night this winter by private detectives, and all the gambling paraphernalia was taken out and the owner . . . sent word to the sheriff's office that if his gambling paraphernalia was not brought back to his place the following day, he would have somebody in jail, as he was paying $1000 a week protection and he would not stand for a double-cross. The next day the paraphernalia was returned to his place.

. . . A bootlegger, was highjacked of 300 cases of whiskey by the sheriff's office, the whiskey being taken to Hialeah and stored in a barn where the bootlegger who lost it located it and went with his own trucks and gang to recover it. While they were loading it the Hialeah police arrived and placed them all under arrest and took their liquor to the Hialeah police station where the sheriff's office came and took 100 cases and sold it to the Biltmore Hotel in Coral Gables. This was reported by the government and they made an investigation but somebody bought them off.

Is There Really a Mafia?

It was to avoid the excessive competition in the Miami–Miami Beach free zone that Meyer Lansky, Capone's urbane successor, chose the Ft. Lauderdale area as his Florida base of operations in the 1940s. Ft. Lauderdale was not as well developed as Miami, but Lansky sensed that it had the same capacity for tolerance that Capone had discovered 45 miles to the south and a few years earlier.

The cause of Lansky's needing an expanded Florida base of operations was the removal of his friend Fulgencio Batista from the Cuban presidency in 1944. Lansky had directed gambling operations for several Cuban hotels with the support of the well-rewarded Batista, but now the generalissimo would be gone. Also, the World War had slowed down the Havana hotel-casino business; the thought of German torpedoes dissuaded gamblers and partygoers from crossing to Cuba via boat.

This first exile of Batista is little-remembered, but the Cuban leader relocated himself in an orange grove near Daytona Beach. Lansky relocated his nightclub apparati to a site in Ft. Lauderdale's Broward County, adjacent to the Gulf Stream Racetrack, and not far from Richard Bolles's original "a good investment beats a lifetime of labor" homesteads. Lansky and his brother Jake, plus partners Vincent Alo (alias Jimmy Blue Eyes), Frank Erickson, and Joe Adonis, among others, opened several gambling clubs or "rug joints"—the Colonial Inn, Greenacres, Club Boheme. The gambling clubs were satellites to The Farm, a bookies' mission control where results from various national racetracks were sent via telephone wires, tabulated, and posted.

Lansky had guessed correctly that illegal gambling in Florida would be less subject to interruption than legal gambling in Cuba, in spite of appearances that might suggest the contrary. During the late 1940s, Ft. Lauderdale was wide open enough so that fifty-two illegal casinos—in addition to the numerous bookie outlets—could operate in and around the Lansky tract.

In Dade County in the 1930s and in Broward in the 1940s, casinos, rug joints, and wire services were no mystery to law enforcement. To see how their operators got away with it, we need only to climb a branch of the family tree of Jim Smith, the Florida attorney general who gives accident of geography speeches. Smith is married to the daughter of a Broward deputy sheriff; Smith's wife's uncle, Walter Clark, ran the sheriff's department. The current attorney general is linked by marriage to the timeless defenders of Florida tolerance: Broward sheriffs not only protected the bookies and casinos with armed deputies; but extra men were deputized, as needed, to carry off the profits in trucks—according to testimony at hearings by the Senate Special Committee to Investigate Organized Crime in Interstate Commerce, held in Miami in 1950.

As recompense, Sheriff Walter Clark was awarded a part interest in the local numbers racket and the slot machines, which is what Batista got for his cooperation back in Cuba—also according to the hearings.

Floridians can go for months and for years patronizing these illegal sites or at least coexisting with them; in the 1940s, there was a bookie's cabana at several prominent Miami Beach hotels, and odds and results were posted on poolside blackboards. Yet every time a crime commission or special task force holds meetings and the testimony makes headlines, the Florida public is said to express shock and disbelief. It is unclear whether "shock and disbelief" is contrived by editors, is disingenuous, or is a genuine reaction of the majority of residents. Perhaps it is only the recent arrivals who are shocked, or perhaps the public exposure of what is privately tolerated releases the Floridians' repressed misgivings.

In any event, Colonel Nutt's discovery of bankers in the booze trade in the 1920s was called "sensational," although it is hard to imagine Miami aghast when the city already was tipped off to his raids. And when Senator Estes Kefauver of Tennessee brought his above-described committee to Miami in 1950, Miami was "amazed" at the revelations of bookies in cabanas, roulette wheels in the nightclubs, and mobsters in the front offices of hotels.

According to some reports, Kefauver might never have come to Miami had not a certain faction of bookies, shut out of the action on Miami Beach, tried to retaliate by working for the election of Governor Fuller Warren on a clean-up-gambling-on-Miami-Beach platform. Senator Kefauver had been concentrating his crime-fighting efforts on cities or states that showed some interest in reform, and Fuller Warren's 1948 victory was popularly interpreted as evidence of Florida's reformist mood. So what may have begun as an intramural squabble among bookies ended in the ouster of all of them, because the Kefauver hearings, and the resulting shock and disbelief, was the gamblers' immediate undoing. Sheriff Clark of Broward County got the worst of the questions. "I let them have what they want for the tourists down here," Clark said. "I was elected on the liberal ticket."

It is possible that Senator Kefauver is indirectly responsible for the fact that 700,000 Cubans now live in the Miami area, through a causal chain that proceeds as follows: The Kefauver hearings riled up enough Floridians to force Lansky out of Broward County; Lansky packed up his paraphernalia and prepared to transfer it back to Havana, a city at least momentarily more wide open than Ft. Lauderdale; Lansky helped convince Batista to return to Cuba; Batista hoped to be elected democratically, but got insecure and reinstalled himself via military coup in 1952; the military government was very unpopular; the unpopularity produced Fidel Castro; the Castro takeover resulted in communism.

If Kefauver hadn't upset the in-state gambling, Lansky might have stayed in Broward, Batista might have stayed in Daytona, Castro would not have needed to start a revolution, and Miami would not be a place where the Spanish-speaking counter help at Kentucky Fried Chicken franchises offers the choice of "orihinal or echtra creepy."

In 1954, a child in St. Petersburg could ask, "Is there really a Mafia?" I was nine years old and had no acquaintance with mobsters. On the fills of Redington Beach, which the maids and gardeners vacated on buses before sundown, felony was unlikely, robbery unique, murder unimaginable—or at least so it seemed. The most threatening potential lawbreakers were retirees with bad eyesight, still licensed to drive. Their cars carried stickers that said "Protected by Pinkerton"; the whole area was safe under the eye of that invisible sentinel. You never saw a Pinkerton, but you figured they must be lurking around everywhere.

Redington Beach was a typical American post-war suburb,

in its apparent isolation from sinister forces. As removed as we were from the great spirit of hustle that opened up the dredged land, we were equally removed from a criminal element. I can hardly recall a physical disturbance, and if I ever knew a felon, I was not aware of it. As a high school student, I thought of myself as a cynic, but that philosophy of disengagement comes out of the suffering of Diogenes, a man who had nothing in common with a resort suburb. I was a cynic who had not suffered; actually, there was no known philosophy to back up the combination of privilege and naïveté, of easy times and hard thoughts, that made up my world view. Existentialism was a popular idea among neighborhood teenagers because it was so imponderable that it could be adopted without consequence. I sampled a few religions, but it was Pinkertonism that sunk in; Pinkertonism marked me, at the mansion on North Bay Road, as a sure narcotics agent.

The three possible sources of lawlessness in the St. Petersburg area as a whole were: (1) those unpredictable interlopers, the native Floridians; (2) the black ghettoes; and (3) the ethnic neighborhoods in the adjacent port city of Tampa. It was fashionable to drive to Tampa for lunch in the Cuban-Spanish restaurants, and then to tour Ybor City, but traffic in the other direction was discouraged, and certain municipalities on the Gulf shore around St. Petersburg tried to keep Tampa's undesirables off the beaches by stopping all cars with Tampa plates and subjecting them to a "license check," bureaucratically closing off their route to the sea.

The question "Is there really a Mafia?" was raised on the news that two Tampa brothers, Santo and Henry Trafficante, were running a bolita game in the St. Petersburg black districts. Bolita was the poor man's trip to Havana, a gambling game played with a burlap bag full of numbered balls. The bag would be tossed in the air to mix the balls, the tosser would then pierce the bag with a knife and extract one ball, which became the winning number. In its more international version, called "Cuba," the winning bolita number was picked in Havana and broadcast over Cuban radio. Long before the Florida middle class had any social or economic dealings with Cubans, long before the drug smugglers took Spanish lessons, the disadvantaged carried on this lively cultural exchange via bolita.

According to the newspapers, Henry Trafficante had tried to bribe a St. Petersburg policeman named Harry Dietrich to protect the local bolita racket. Dietrich had played along through bottles of whiskey and free suits and finally a brand-new yellow Mercury convertible. The convertible was formally awarded to Dietrich in the alley behind the Penguin Lounge in Tampa. The policeman wore a long coat that concealed a wire recorder, an early and primitive version of a tape machine. Dietrich took the front seat on the passenger side, Henry Trafficante sat in the driver's place, Santo Trafficante got into the back. Santo was breathing on the policeman's neck while the policeman bounced up and down as if he had to go to the bathroom, trying to squeak the seat springs to drown out the squeaking noises coming out of the recorder.

Dietrich's one-man investigation led to sensational revelations: thirty-eight St. Petersburg blacks and the two Trafficantes were arrested. "Shocked To Core by Testimony of Corruption," the headline said; the reason Dietrich worked solo was that half the police force and some of his superiors were already on the take. St. Petersburg, with its limited imagination for the possibilities of crime, could no better measure the stature of its Tampa captives than the Lilliputians could measure their giant visitor. From the bench, the judge who had been shocked to the core called the two Trafficante brothers "rats who crept out of the sewers of Tampa to contaminate our town." The newspapers described the

Trafficantes as "bolita kingpins" or "Tampa hoodlums." Nowhere in the coverage, as I have researched it, is there a mention of the fact that Santo Trafficante and his father before him operated Havana casinos for Meyer Lansky, who had returned to Cuba after the Batista takeover in 1952.

Santo Trafficante was on leave from Havana, come home to settle family affairs in the illness and death of his father, when he bumbled into this bribery trap through the apparent mistake of his less-adept brother, Henry. The arrest must have been infuriating, because the St. Petersburg bolita game was a sidelight, as compared to the action in Cuba.

Both Trafficantes were convicted. "A Great Day for the Tortoise," the editorial in the *Tampa Tribune* said. "Justice often moves like the tortoise but in . . . Florida courts this week it finally overtook racketeers who had played the hare's role for a discouragingly long time."

Santo's conviction was soon overturned by higher authorities with a more cosmic philosophy than Pinkertonism. The hoodlum of my pre-adolescence, the rat who crawled out of the sewers of Tampa, later represented the country as the liaison between the Mafia and the CIA. It was at a private meeting behind a paramilitary fashion show at the Miami Beach Fontainebleau Hotel in 1961 that Santo Trafficante was handed the poison to put into Fidel Castro's soup.

The Latins

In 1959, a few Cuban exiles found their way to St. Petersburg, resulting in an improvement in the Spanish classes. Our junior high school teacher was from Georgia and could not have talked her way through a Tijuana hotel, but by the time we reached the higher grades, we were taught by an ex-Cuban university professor in exile. He was a new Cuban, a victim of Communism, as distinguished from the old Cubans, victims of colonialism, who decades earlier had migrated to Tampa's Ybor City but never had reached the Spanish departments.

The two groups of Cubans had little affinity. Tampa Cubans, the citizens of Ybor City, identified more closely with Spain, the colonizers from whom they originally had escaped. Tampa Cubans were blue-collar people and cigar workers; they rolled blunts and panatellas to the rhythm of the voice of a lector, who sat above them in a pulpit, reading the poems of José Martí. We liked their restaurants, although we distrusted them for certain unusual practices, such as the selling of leeches in the drugstores as over-the-counter medicine.

The old Cubans, the new Cuban reinforcements, and the

stories of vanishing conquistadores told in the schoolbooks and on the metal historic plaques inspired a local interest in Latin American affairs. Latin American studies was my college major. I expected, someday, to be a foreign correspondent. Through the *St. Petersburg Times*, where I worked during three summers, I got a summer job on a newspaper in Chile. Later, I took a post-graduate year in Ecuador, and spent additional years in Ecuador in the Peace Corps. My Spanish was nearly fluent by the time I became exasperated with Latin America and moved to Washington to write for the magazine that in 1972 sent me to the Republican convention on Miami Beach. Miami was the foreign post from which I had unintentionally prepared myself to correspond.

For during all the years that I studied Latin American history and wondered how best the gringo could influence life below the border, Miami had been filling up with exiles—their migration resulting in part from the Florida machinations about which I knew nothing.

"Miamuh" it used to be called before the Cubans arrived in 1959. Until the final fall of Batista, one could down-home one's way into the heart of town. Southern and somewhat moribund, it boasted one or two gangster-connected banks, a few nightclubs, some shipping. Tourists were likely to bypass it in favor of Miami Beach. The twenty thousand Hispanics who lived in the area, plus a handful of Latin American dictators scattered about with their national treasuries, were lost in the drawls.

The revolution brought 3,000 of the wealthiest Cubans, mostly of the Batista party, who transferred here in early 1959; 7,000 wealthy but non-Batista Cubans followed later that year; 150,000 professional and middle-class Cubans landed in a continuous airlift until the flights were canceled after the Cuban missile crisis; 245,000 Cubans of diverse backgrounds signed up for the flights after they resumed in 1965.

This amounted to 400,000 Cubans in six years, descending on a county whose entire population at the start of the exodus had not reached a million. It was as if Leonard Rosen had given all his salesmen Spanish lessons, and all the buyers moved in at once. In 1960, Hispanics in the region added up to 4 percent of the population; by 1970, they comprised 23 percent of Miami alone. Estranged gringos began to migrate themselves, south to Kendall or farther south to Homestead, north to Ft. Lauderdale or farther north to Vero Beach, places where they still sold fried chicken in English.

Cuban immigrants did not fit any of Emma Lazarus' categories: they were not your tired, your hungry, your poor, they were your energetic, your well-nourished, your middle class, yearning to be free of Castro, but not necessarily free of dictators in general. Many had supported Batista. They were different from the nineteenth-century Europeans who cherished America as a solution to their problems; for the Cubans, America was a solution but also a cause of their problems, the U.S. having manipulated their politics for decades, the U.S. being in part responsible for their having to come here. The Cuban ambivalence toward their hosts (especially after we abandoned them at the Bay of Pigs), combined with their energetic arrogance, did not produce the hat-in-hand attitude.

Unlike the Italians or the Irish, the Poles or the Hungarians, the Latvians or the Italians, or even the Vietnamese, the Cubans expected to return home in a few days, then weeks, then months, never more than months; the invasion, for a decade, was imminent. Looking constantly over their shoulders, diverted half the time by the upcoming invasion, and, until recently, never imagining that they would stay, the Cubans established themselves as quickly and as successfully as any exiles in history. Doctors and lawyers worked two shifts in grocery stores while studying for their U.S. licenses, businessmen started over in the tomato fields of Homestead and went on to become millionaires. Together the Cubans excelled on their own terms, coaxing an international city out of a Southern town, and although their prosperity has been exaggerated—Miami still being one of the poorer large cities in the country in income per capita—the Cubans have made exceptional progress. Perhaps all immigrants should convince themselves they are just visiting.

I was working in Washington when Miami Cubans brought Latin America into White House politics, via the tape on the Watergate doors. Watergate was the unsolved mystery of the summer of 1972. From Washington, the Watergate story began to sound more and more like a Nixon psychosis and less and less like a rerun of the Bay of Pigs. We prefer to remember Watergate as Nixon's moral problem and not as our Latin American policy coming back on itself, back through Florida. Somehow, it is less disturbing to think of it that way, even though the soldiers in the Watergate brigade were veterans of the Cuban raiding parties, some of the same CIA people were implicated in both adventures, and the case officer for Watergate was novelist Howard Hunt, who wrote the constitution for the New Cuba from a safe house in Miami's Coconut Grove.

Many of the Miami angles had developed at the moment of my personal transfer. Now I was living on Miami Beach, having just moved from Washington, speaking Spanish, in the perfect position to participate in the greatest scoop of the century, the best sources of which were collected a few miles across Biscayne Bay. Instead, I was installed in the upstairs bedroom of the North Bay Road mansion, listening to Ink Spots records, learning how to play backgammon, and watching the invertebrate sea creatures fight it out in the downstairs aquarium.

The Florida recreative spirit seemed to be at odds with the extraordinary muckraking opportunities that its exile politics had created.

I remained in poolside semiretirement, halfheartedly pursuing extraneous assignments, when other journalists who stayed at the mansion during the conventions returned to investigate leads they had picked up in Washington, leads that took them into Cuban neighborhoods where metal grilles covered the picture windows and plaster saints were installed in carports, where big dogs and chain-link fences provided security around tiny houses, where speedboats were parked like cars along the streets, where sidewalk cafés served coffee essence in paper pill cups, where lemon and pineapple vendors worked the stoplights, hawking the fruit in Spanish under Spanish billboards, where furniture stores featured red velour settees and aluminum hard-edged tables, where movie marquees advertised Libertad LeBlanc and other stars you never heard of.

One of the journalists is my friend Taylor Branch. With northern dedication, Branch came back to interview two Cubans who participated in the break-in: Rolando Martínez and Bernard Barker. Barker and Martínez introduced Branch to other CIA-trained Cubans, and Branch drove back to the mansion each evening to discuss his findings. Cubans were the talk of the pool. There were at least fifty different splinter groups waging war against Communists, Branch said, the supporters of Communism having expanded in their frustration to include the *Miami Herald*, many American politicians, the FBI, and bureaucrats from various state, local, and federal agencies.

The more Branch talked to the Cuban activists, the less he understood about them. People who called themselves by one name would on the next occasion use another, Cubans who appeared to be compatible would privately accuse each other of being Castro agents; there were two and three interpretations of every basic fact. It should have been a clue that the mansion on North Bay Road was a trivialized version of Miami at large, but I wasn't listening too closely, being absorbed in the domestic intrigues of the mansion itself. Branch's stories of Cuban agents who said a lot but revealed little were recounted in the presence of suspected in-house drug dealers who communicated in the same way.

In the early 1960s, about the time that the subdividers were in high vigor, when serpentariums were used as locations for land sales, when the aquarium on Collins Avenue likewise wasn't simply an aquarium, when every gracious bellhop was on clandestine assignment for Gulf American or General Development Corporation, various Miami shipping companies were not really shipping companies and various electronics companies were not electronics companies, they were political bug shops, fronts for the CIA. From 1960 to 1964, the CIA was the largest employer in town, $50 million a year, three hundred domestic operatives, fifty-four dummy corporations, hundreds of cars, psychologists, boats, safe houses all over the place.

Hundreds of young Cuban men had been trained by the intelligence organization, that was their naturalization course. During the early 1960s, when the idea was to dispose of Castro and to return to the island in weeks or months, the CIA was the crucial domestic agency for the Cubans. It hand-picked a Cuban government in exile, it contracted with Hunt to write the constitution. Miami had the largest CIA station in the world, but more important than the size was its designation. The Miami CIA station was the only one in the United States that ever got foreign status. It existed above the domestic rules, it played the game as it is played in Santiago or Marrakesh. Before any of the Miami gringos decided that they were no longer living in America, the city was defined as alien by its controlling agency.

The statistics alone cannot begin to reveal the extent of CIA influence, because for every connection that showed overtly, three other connections were made underground. According to Branch, each American CIA case officer had ten subordinate Cuban officers, each Cuban officer had twenty to thirty men under his charge, there were thousands of Cubans drawing expenses or drawing a salary. The CIA subsidized newspapers, marinas, fishing companies, stores—just about every kind of business in the exile community.

If the intent was to subvert Castro and to retake Cuba, the result was that the CIA gave the young Cuban leadership a government-supported lesson in how to subvert the American system. Before and beyond the Bay of Pigs, the CIA directed the Cubans to carry on a secret war. None of this was authorized above-board and the Cubans knew it; most of what their guiding agency told them to do was in violation of the U.S. neutrality laws. Several hundred of the most energetic exiles were issued double or triple identities, false passports, code names, illegal automatic weapons, and phony driver's licenses.

The *Miami Herald* overlooked the CIA presence, so the paramilitary exiles were immune from the scrutiny of the press. The seventeen area police agencies gave the closet soldiers virtual immunity from prosecution as well. Cubans could carry machine guns in their cars and would not be arrested; if they were arrested they called their case officers and the charges were dropped. They could get easy divorces. For them, the mundane transactions in Miami were as facilitated as they would have been in Havana if the right person had been in power. There was no culture shock here; the CIA had imposed a banana republic above the regular institutions of government. For many Cubans, this was their first experience in America; what else could they believe but that false passports, code names, and phony driver's licenses were the American way?

◆◆◆◆◆

Miami at large was well-trained to abet a secret war. Its residents were accustomed to seeing casinos that in theory did not exist, and bookmakers in the cabanas of Miami Beach hotels who in theory were not in business, and so why should they have questioned the gunboats on the Miami River or the airplanes painted in green-and-brown camouflage at the Miami airport, or the men with military rifles crawling through fields at the edge of the Everglades?

The officially sanctioned raids against Castro, which lasted into the mid-1960s, gave way to a period of incendiary freelance. The C-4 plastique once destined for Cuba was attached instead to buildings in Miami—to FBI headquarters, inside the bathroom at the state attorney's office—by CIA-trained exiles angry that the U.S. had stopped supporting their cause. Then there was an international period, when CIA-trained Cubans began to leave Miami, taking their ordnance, their intelligence, and their Florida training elsewhere, forming murderous little cadres all over the globe. It was this global Cuban influence that culminated in Watergate and the perplexing challenge for journalists like my friend Branch: just who was subverting whom?

Branch's stories were fascinating but somewhat otherworldly. I felt they had nothing whatever to do with the average nominal Floridian, who in this instance was about to leave Miami Beach and return to the land.

But then in 1974, we came back to search for building materials for our Everglades City house in the old Miami Beach neighborhood. There was a big salvage sale at the house at 4609 Pine Tree Drive, not far from North Bay Road. Was it dumb chance that this house had mob connections that went as far back as the bolita games of St. Petersburg, or that plots to kill Castro were developed within its walls? Is there a statistical significance in the fact that such a salvage site, picked at random from the newspapers, would have these antecedents?

The history of the Pine Tree Drive house came out later, in *The Fish Is Red,* a book about the CIA-Mafia alliance. It had been owned by Venezuelan dictator Marcos Pérez Jiménez, who escaped here with his national treasury; Carlos Marcello, the Mafia boss of New Orleans, was rumored to be Pérez's silent partner. The dictator's daughter was married to one of Meyer Lansky's casino managers; all three men—Pérez Jiménez, Lansky, and Marcello—were enlisted in the anti-Castro crusades. Exploding cigars were first considered here; perhaps it was the very place that Santo Trafficante, rat from the sewers of Tampa, planned his poison soup.

The invisible army and the invisible gambling joints had interlocking directorates that went back as far as Meyer Lansky and spread across Florida to St. Petersburg, and now they had reached us through a yard sale. The Pine Tree Drive mansion was being demolished. Susan and I pried out the kitchen cabinets, pulled cedar from the closets, extracted cypress windows, hauled away three sinks, and unhinged some beautiful French doors.

Our new house in Everglades City, open to nature's breezes, sunk in Collier fill, connected to Rosen's drainage through local aquifers, was constructed of materials previously owned by a dictator and a mobster and used by clandestine operatives. We built their residue around us. Mob cedar was in our bathroom, we cut our vegetables on their Formica, we looked out the dictator's windows, we washed our hands in his sink.

In 1976, the salvage from the Venezuelan dictator's house was nailed or bolted into the Everglades City context. We looked out of Marcos Pérez Jiménez's old windows (not knowing, then, that they had belonged to him), and across

Barron Collier's river, watching the pelicans, watching the migratory buzzards, tending the tomato garden on the former golf course, suspicious, by then, about the nighttime runs of the fishing boats, when characters from the salvage entered the space.

These characters didn't reach us directly, but through my friend Branch, who still lived in Washington and wrote about the machinations from up there. A bomb had killed the former Chilean ambassador and a young companion in Washington. Branch heard that the identity of the murderer might be revealed by a Cuban exile jailed in Venezuela on allegations that he, too, planted a bomb; one that blew up a Cuban airliner a few weeks earlier, killing seventy-three people.

The leads that could be traced from Watergate through Miami were now twisted around a worldful of unsolved homicides, toppled governments, assassinations; to me, it still sounded like second-rate Graham Greene. But Branch was flying to Venezuela to talk to the accused airline bomber who supposedly had information about the Washington explosion. He needed a translator, and my Peace Corps Spanish, seven years unpracticed, was the best he could get at short notice. I didn't want to go for long, as Susan was about to have a baby.

We got our passports in Miami and, at the last minute, a better translator: Hilda Inclan, a Cuban-born reporter for the *Miami News,* was headed for Caracas herself and decided to join us. On the same plane were two Miami policemen, one the son-in-law of Watergate burglar Rolando Martínez, plus two Miami state attorneys. They knew Branch from his earlier investigations, and took a nervous interest in what we might be doing. They didn't say what they were doing, but somehow we all knew we were on the same trail. Seeing four representatives of Miami law enforcement materialize on this random flight to Venezuela made me guess that the city and the terrorists it trained were still very closely connected.

The Cuban we expected to interview in the jail was Orlando Bosch, the terrorist pediatrician. "Terrorist" was a word from gringo editorials; blowing up a Castro airliner, for which Bosch was accused, was not regarded as a crime among Miami exiles who believed that all Communists, including women and children, deserved to die.

Branch had some newspaper clips of bombings for which the pediatrician had already been convicted, from that period of incendiary freelance when buildings in Miami had blown up. "Bosch Arrested in Shelling of Polish Freighter," the 1968 headline from the *Miami Herald* read: the pediatrician was out at the edge of the MacArthur Causeway that connected Miami with Miami Beach, aiming a shoulder-held bazooka at ships bound for Cuba, missing the target, arrested by the FBI.

There were other clips; Bosch in a Florida prison, a picture of his cadaverous face behind bars, caught in such an intense grimace that the face looked as if it had died in a scream. The star witness against Bosch in this bazooka case was another CIA-trained Cuban bomber named Ricardo Morales, who had been granted immunity for his explosions in return for his cooperation against Bosch's.

Somehow, the relative positions of these two Cubans were duplicated in Venezuela: Bosch behind bars again, and Morales outside, working with law enforcement, with some police agency in Caracas. Branch expected that reaching Orlando Bosch might be difficult, but he was comforted by the presence of Morales, whom he had once met in Miami and considered our ally in reserve.

We never met Bosch, but we met Morales; Morales introduced himself by breaking into our hotel room at 4 A.M., six hours after we landed in Caracas. It wasn't much of an intrusion, in comparison with tortures and bombings and the disappearance of thousands of leftists, but it was the most terrifying thing that ever happened to me. Ridiculous the way it began: the three of us, Branch, Inclan, and I, were harassed by airport security, then our car was followed to the hotel, then we saw the armed guards stationed in the bushes, then there was trouble with the phones and our calls never got out, then we started to wander out of the lobby and were tailed. Afraid to be caught in some dark alley with our pursuer, we returned to our room, where we spent the rest of the night trying to figure out whom we had upset.

The Morales appearance was the most frightening of all because it was so unexpected. In all the confusing tales of double and triple identities, the only certainty down here was that Morales was the person to call.

In fact, we had tried to call Morales in the middle of the night, after we failed to reach the embassy or the international operator. Hilda Inclan, our journalist companion, thought she had seen Morales after we had deplaned, Morales embracing the two Miami policemen and the two state attorneys who had been on the flight. He didn't greet us then—perhaps he hadn't seen us—but now he attacked in our predawn stupor, scooping our passports off the dresser, barking orders like a drill sergeant, yelling "pack up and get downstairs," "move, move, move." Branch was perplexed; Hilda Inclan was more indignant than perplexed; I was more afraid than indignant, and I cursed the Peace Corps Spanish that got me here.

Branch recognized Morales from their earlier interview, back in Miami, when Branch had been following up the leads from Watergate. The Cuban exile looked fifteen years older now, although only four years had elapsed between that earlier interview and this unexpected one. Morales was about five-foot-eight, with a full face, a slight paunch, graying hair, and pronounced bags under his eyes. The double and triple identities had caught up to us here: Morales would not admit to having ever spoken to Branch or Inclan, he ignored all questions, he marshaled us out of the room, down the stairs, through the check-out, and into a waiting car.

Being trapped in the car with Morales's armed assistants, and driven from the hotel to an unknown destination, I reflected on Susan's pregnancy, on the beauty of the Everglades, and on the stupidity of nonfiction journalism, since Graham Greene could invent much better and at no risk. I imagined them taking us out and shooting us and claiming it was an accident. That Venezuela was a democracy that was no comfort in this car; Venezuelan democracy was not as reassuring as U.S. democracy, and U.S. democracy had trained Morales to fight in its name. I kept looking out the window, expecting us to turn up some rural road, mortally relieved when we stopped at the airport, where the three of us were deposited in a back room that seemed to be a headquarters for undercover police.

Branch was full of more practical speculations that took him back to the little coffee shops on Miami's Southwest Eighth Street. A complex oration on Miami's Cuban intrigues my friend could give extemporaneously; I had never paid as much attention to it as now. Somehow, we were trapped between two Cubans, both graduates of the CIA naturalization course, one whom we wanted to interview but could not, the other whom we might have desired to interview, but now hoped never to see again. We doubted that we would be so fortunate, since Ricardo Morales still had our passports.

Maybe Morales had detained us to keep us from talking to his enemy, Orlando Bosch. That was one of Branch's theories, discarded on the grounds that it was Morales who had invited Bosch to Venezuela in the first place, suggesting that the two Cubans had made up. Maybe Morales had detained us to keep us from talking to his friend. Then again, it had been Morales that ordered the jailing of Bosch in Venezuela, suggesting that the rapprochement was an illusion and that Morales had duped Bosch twice, once in the Florida courtroom and now here. Maybe the two of them were in subterranean cahoots.

There were a dozen corollary suppositions, all having to do with Miami, the Miami-CIA entanglement that was recreated here. Whatever happened between Morales and Bosch, and between Morales and us, came out of the Miami secret war, the spy training, the bomb trials during the period of incendiary freelance. The two Miami policemen and two state's attorneys whom we saw on the plane were evidence enough of Florida's role in our predicament. Hilda Inclan suspected that they had come to Venezuela to court Morales, to seek his cooperation in yet another Florida trial of yet another exile bomber with whom Morales had an imponderable relationship.

Our theorizing in the room at the airport, where we had been deposited, was interrupted by Ricardo Morales himself, who arrived to invite us to breakfast, as graciously as if we were guests at his hotel. He must have known that we despised him for what he had done to us, yet he managed to play the charming and genial host, so sure of his power over us, of our fear of him, that he walked us through open corridors to a public restaurant, knowing that we would not grab phones, run, or scream that we were victims of a kidnap, knowing that we would follow him like lambs.

The four of us sat at a table in a busy cafeteria. Morales and Branch did most of the talking, after having thought through our execution, I could barely swallow my eggs. Morales was genial and expansive, a typical Cuban in that way, but at the point he sensed our relaxation, he called us liars and bullied us back into insecurity. At close range, he held up his deception without flinching, denying that he ever heard of Orlando Bosch, denying that he knew Branch, denying that he kicked us out of a hotel room, denying it all with such self-assured vehemence that I began to wonder if we were not deluded, instead of him.

Morales asked me who I was, I told him I lived in the Everglades, but by his look I know he didn't believe it. I think he pegged me as something more commonplace, as just another spy.

He spoke excellent English; he said he got all his information from *Time* magazine, and he told a joke about how the Cincinnati Reds not only won the World Series that year, but that the Reds were also winning the world. That he was at war with Communists was the only specific thing he admitted. Without saying so, Morales came across as our defender in a conflict beyond our comprehension, that if only we could understand what we were up against, we would not blame him.

After breakfast, he redeposited us in the little room, guarded by supernumeraries in reflecto sunglasses and shoulder holsters, whom we feared much less than the Cuban who had flashed no gun. The goons forced us onto airplanes after a public tug-of-war at the departure gates. We had wanted to create enough commotion so that higher authorities than Morales would liberate us from his domain, but that never happened, and we were expelled from the country. I was the most anxious to leave; I took the first plane; Branch and Inclan resisted longer. They were pushed around by more gun-toting assistants and were flown out a few hours later.

Why Morales kicked us out of Venezuela is still a mystery. I was fascinated by the Cuban exile—maybe I respected him, perhaps I even liked him, certainly I feared him. He came out of plots heard by our cedar and our sinks, a Florida-raised Cuban hybrid for whom a Florida expert on Latin American studies was no match.

The Fourth Dimension

By the time our baby could walk, Everglades City was abuzz with Skil saws and the hammering of pile drivers. Prosperity had brought back the developers. The across-the-river tract was still safe from bridge permits, but a consortium from Naples had purchased the Captain's Table, the hotel resort project that had sat in bankruptcy at the edge of the town circle, threatening would-be speculators for two decades.

The Captain's Table bar and restaurant reopened. They occupied separate rooms in this predictable Florida-style complex; both rooms were paneled in native cypress. The bar was outfitted like the hold of a ship, with sloping walls, red lights to port, green lights to starboard. Fishermen in a mood to celebrate began to give up the old 4 A.M. wake-up schedule and their day-long toil on the stone-crab boats in favor of a hitch on the Captain's Table bar-ship, from which they reached 4 A.M. via the nighttime direction.

As the bar and restaurant got popular, the owners announced that they could not survive on food and liquor sales alone, a developer maxim that goes back as far as Carl Fisher, and that leads to the bulldozing of property and to the inevitable sales to retirees.

These particular developers decided to put up condominiums. Their proposal came through the zoning and planning boards and was sent on to the city council. It was a still a council of nonsmugglers, solid citizens like my friend Snapper Butler, men with strong opinions but with a collective reluctance to disappoint. The council would approve most anything in principle and agree to study it and take a vote at the next special meeting; then, if there was opposition at that meeting, yet another meeting would be required, and both opponents and proponents of any project always were convinced that the council was on their side.

Since the developers planned to install their condos on already dredged land, there was no argument from the mangrove-lovers; and since they had already opened the Captain's Table, they had made many local friends. The "Whoa, Yankee" sign over on Chokoloskee Island still spoke for the people, but the local resistance to a new cluster of outsiders was softened up in the nautical bar.

After a few special meetings, the project was approved, the land adjacent to the restaurant cleared off, a swimming pool dug, and the buildings shipped in on flatbed trucks. This was Everglades City's first sight of condominiums, if you don't count the old six-unit apartment house over on Hibiscus Avenue, whose owners had wanted to convert.

The buildings were the kind usually found in low-cost housing projects, pressed wood siding and granulated spray stucco interiors, contents already in place, art already attached to the walls. A batch of these prefab units was set up on stilts, garnished with palm trees, and it looked very nice. The siding on these thirty or so new condominiums had hardly begun to weather before a second batch was proposed, identical in every respect except the form of ownership. The second batch was called "River Wilderness, a time-share resort."

A new concept, the developers called it, and they took to it before the condo units sold out. No doubt they would have bypassed condos altogether had they known of time-sharing earlier. For time-sharing transported them beyond the two dimensions of subdivisions, beyond the three dimensions of high-rises, beyond Pythagoras, beyond Descartes, into Einsteinian realms. It was the three-dimensional crisis of too many condos, a glut of Cartesian slots, that inspired time-share; out of the vastness of distressed real estate came this idea of ownership of property in space *and* time, more specifically in two-week intervals, the buyer taking legal possession at the intersection of a unit and his chosen two-week span, controlling that intersection for eternity.

Time-share is everywhere: Europe, Colorado, Massachusetts; but Florida has the most of it, half the units in the country are sold here. Space and time created an inexhaustible supply of salable parcels: a simple 50-unit motel, reorganized in this way, became 1,250 units—twenty-five two-week intervals for each room. It was the culmination of parcelizing that began with subdividers and went skyward when the dredges were stopped. Nothing could be denser, in buyers per cubic volume, than a high-rise time-share building; a cluster of such buildings could accommodate every vacationer on earth.

The new geometry improved the economics, which is why any sensible developer would prefer the second batch of prefabs to the first. The total cost of one trucked-in unit was, say, $10,000, or perhaps more with the foundation and landscaping. As condos, the units were selling for $30,000 each; but in space-time they returned $100,000, twenty-five two-week intervals at $2,000 a week. In an eight-unit project at River Wilderness, time-share might gross $1.2 million, where condos might gross $360,000.

A caravan of time-share salesmen reached Everglades City en masse, their arrival answered the question: What ever happened to all those refugees from the Rosen land sales, put out of business by the Federal Trade Commission and the environmental movement? They were our newest neighbors, stippled among the smugglers, hard-drinking and cynical desperadoes of marketing, called out of bartending or car sales to be rejoined to real estate, like the jazz musicians of New Orleans brought back from the docks. The manager of the Captain's Table Resort was himself an ex-swamp salesman from the Remuda Ranch grants, he told me of the great migration of the installment-lot promoters to this new opportunity, beyond the limits of the federal and state regulations that foiled the linear subdividers, out on the space-age frontier of Florida sales.

Time-share revived the WATS-line jockeys, the barkers, the bounty-hunting of the bellhops; the *Miami Herald* reported that Bernie Horowitz, convicted in an earlier scheme to attact buyers to subdivisions, might be running a time-share vacation bureau from his jail cell. On the beaches of St. Petersburg, attractive young men dressed up like Santa Clauses and carrying huge sacks of free cameras stopped beachcombers, pointed to nearby buildings, and asked, "Do you want to own a piece of that?" It was the old Gulf American formula: 50 percent of the cost of a space-time unit was spent on convincing a client to buy it. There were no free weekends in space-time, only invitations to take the tour and to pick up prizes.

Invitations to time-share resorts filled Florida mailboxes, and mailboxes across the nation, if one can judge by the collection in ours: mailgrams, speedograms, instant lotto award sheets, universal cables, urgent instagrams, letters that look as if they came from lawyers, first notices, second notices, even a hand-written note from a woman in Ft. Lauderdale, all happy to inform us that we may have won a gas grill, a Chevette, a portable color TV, microwave oven, stereo system, gold chain, but more likely the plastic camera, the ballpoint pen, or the costume jewelry, the specific prize to be revealed later:

> Mr. Rothchild, enclosed you will find a sealed envelope. Whatever you do . . . do not open this envelope, until you are in the presence of a Key Largo awards director. Tampering with the envelope immediately voids this offer. Your specific award is determined by the contents of the envelope. One of the nine vacation time awards listed above is yours. The awards have been divided into three groups. To discover which awards are in your group, call immediately, 1-800-328-1590 and give your group number. Then schedule an appointment to visit and inspect Key Largo and to receive your award. You must bring the sealed envelope and this mailogram with you.

The undesirability of having two weeks forever in a low-cost housing project on the wrong side of this rowdy little town full of drug smugglers was obvious on cold inspection; the buildings didn't look too permanent to me, and then there was the matter of dealing with hundreds of owners scattered about the country or the world after the developers sold out and left. What if somebody breaks something and files a lawsuit? What if people stop paying their annual maintenance? Where is the resale market? These were a few of the questions that formed an insurmountable barrier between common sense and such a purchase. But then people had bought swamps down the road at Remuda Ranch, and by the look of the traffic through the River Wilderness time-share office, people were buying this. Even in the mosquito season, we saw clients tour the units and sprint to their cars, slapping like Keystone Kops, followed by the salesmen's promise: "A mosquito district is soon to be approved."

Time-share was a chance to be Rosenized, to experience the techniques that sold instant cities and made subdivisions out of swamps. The salesmen came back, as everything in Florida seems to come back, in perfect and recognizable form.

The tour of River Wilderness we declined; we knew too much about the units to be impressed. But later, we signed up for a tour of an old motel on the beach in Boca Raton, near Ft. Lauderdale, near the site of Richard Bolles's original swampsteads, a fallen little motel now revived in the fourth dimension and renamed Enchanted Isle.

There was a corridor for an entranceway, and then a waiting room for all the people who had come for the inspection tour and the free prizes. It was a Greyhound bus crowd, minimum-wage types and some blacks, the old "X" restrictions for subdivisions lifted for outer space. Each couple was given an appointment with a salesperson who worked from a ceramic patio table with a round umbrella.

We got Mary—mid-twenties, debauched, chubby, tired. She had transferred to time-sharing out of bartending in St. Petersburg. She was too young to have sold Rosen property, but she traveled with other salesmen from those days; it was a nomadic tribe that moved from one motel to another, selling out one place, camping in the next, exhausting the dimension, getting their commission checks on the spot. She wasn't a real estate agent; she didn't have to be a real estate agent, the state had given some sort of dispensation on this, she was trained by the industry.

"Just how much do these units at Enchanted Isle cost?" we asked Mary as we sat down at her patio table and after we had finished the biographical preliminaries. She covered her ring with her other hand and answered in parable: "Would you buy this ring from me without having examined it? What does price mean if you don't know what you are buying?"

"What are we buying?" we asked Mary. She said it wasn't a matter of what we were buying, it was a matter of frame of reference, she wanted us to relax and be happy, we were her guests. "Think of a perfect vacation," Mary said. "It could be anywhere, France, England, the Caribbean, Aspen." She produced a photo album with pictures of mountains, European cities, London, beaches on the Bahamas, ski lodges, and told us to transport ourselves to these faraway and wonderful destinations that all offered time-share units, units with which Florida owners could trade.

We strolled with Mary along the beautiful Atlantic beachfront while she talked about the scenery of the Alps. It was the Florida dream she was trained to induce, that dream that produced Moorish castles and Italian canals, signs that promised Vermont landscape, and salesmen who could point your eye across the Everglades and ask you to see Kansas. It was not these surroundings Mary was selling, although the beach behind the motel was among the most pleasant of stretches; it was the hope for something else, a vision of a future time and place, no different in essence than the vision of Miami Beach conjured up by Gulf American salesmen on the moonscape of Cape Coral.

Is this the crux of it—that through the wetlands, the subdivisions that allude to non-existent hills and trees, and into outer space, Florida presents itself not as property, substance, meets and bounds, but as opportunity to escape, to be transported? It is not reality we get, reality is deficient even when reality is agreeable. Does this come from Florida's ancient insecurity as a land mass or from notions that paradise should be unattainable? Whatever the reason, we weren't seeing the motel unit, we weren't seeing the Atlantic, we were seeing mountains rising from Mary's dream book.

Mary had forty-five minutes to keep us enchanted. We asked to go back and she kept walking us farther from the units, finally she admitted she was not allowed to return us any earlier. She deposited us in the room that might be ours for two weeks forever, so that we could touch the silverware and open the closets and discuss the colors of drapes, and then she left us at the door of the solidifiers.

Dreams of escape were only half of this Florida vision; the other half was crasser. The closer we got to the matter of the contract the more intolerable our hosts became. Here were the auto-showroom bullies from the hard days of swamp marketing, arm-twisting couples fresh from their forty-five-minute pleasant journeys, telling the couples that time-share is a good investment.

This is the fantasy that really sells time-share, the one that sold palmetto scrub in the 1920s and lots you couldn't find with jeeps and half-tracks in the 1950s and hives of condos in the 1970s—the fantasy that somewhere out in the vastness of time-space there is enough demand to make a resale market, that someday an $8,000 two-week slice of a motel room (what this one cost) would be worth twice, four times, ten times more. Greed is the ultimate appeal, a little extra something for nothing; greed is the key ingredient in the alchemy of suckers. Florida is not unique to it, but seems to evoke it more successfully than any place I know; this is where people hope to give the slip to their predicaments.

Sign up now, the salesmen said, or lose the chance, as if at these rates there wouldn't be an infinite supply of units. When we refused to listen any further, Mary came back to throw the little plastic camera and the box of costume jewelry ("These aren't worth anything," she said) at our feet, and to revile us as: "Moochers who won't even pay for your own vacation place."

Later, I discovered that the state's role in this fourth dimension of property sales hadn't changed since its regulation of the third dimension and before that, the second. In support of the multi-million-dollar time-share industry, the Florida legislature passed an exemption from the ten-day-waiting period for the normal real estate closing, so that time-share clients could be solidified on the spot. The state even collected a 50-cent fee for each time-share unit sold. The director of time-share enforcement in Tallahassee told me that time-share abuses were the work of a few unscrupulous salesmen, bad apples who ruined the reputation of the rest. "Beauty is truth, truth beauty—that is all ye know on earth, and all ye need to know"—so said Keats, so said Leonard Rosen, so says Florida.

Only in 1983, three years after the flatbeds brought the first time-share units to Everglades City—three years of an embarrassing and profitable spectacle in which Florida got its customary national black eye—did the state revoke the exemption from the waiting period, disallow the mailbox sweepstakes, force the time-share industry into better repute, and, not surprisingly, send it into recession.

I was on the planning board that approved River Wilderness, one of those residents who winked as the caravan came through. My sense of community did not extend to these buyers—they were a source of amusement, of taxes, and a way to keep the local restaurant open. Most, we figured, bought units in the Everglades so they could trade with Colorado or with the Alps. Those who owned space-time in the bug season we doubted would ever been seen in town again. For that matter, neither would we.

Familiar Latitude

Whether our exodus from Everglades City, in late 1980, was caused more by the spectacle of fishermen with coke habits, the auto crashes of drivers on Quaaludes into the local bridge, my having lost a city council election by one vote, the children getting too old to go to a backwoods school, the time-share units, the neighbors going to prison, or the fact that the little village, in spite of it all, had begun to bore us, I don't know. It was during the 1980 *Mariel* boatlift, when half the fishing fleet that smuggled pot and hated Cubans took off for Cuba on the expectation of $2,000 per delivered refugee, that I realized that Everglades City was no retreat from anything, and if we were going to be surrounded by smugglers, speculators, and Cuban deliveries, it might as well be in a place with decent restaurants and first-run movies.

We rented our homemade house to a time-share salesman who sold units here and in the Cayman Islands, which seemed better advised than renting it to a local smuggler, although really it made no difference, since the salesman's girlfriend entertained all the cocaine dealers while we were away. They were good tenants, they even cleaned the oven.

Neither Susan nor I had a regular job, and so the five of us could have gone anywhere, back to New York, back to Washington, west to California, south to the Bahamas, east to London. Instead, we opted for a return to Miami, only 80 miles away and much less distant from Everglades City, in outlook and in sources of revenue, than we had imagined it to be in 1973, as we drove in the other direction.

No longer could I play the ingenue, untouched by the surroundings and ignorant of the implications. With full knowledge of the anarchism, the inelegance, the yawning venality of it all, still we chose for our next home the same latitude and the same old founding muckspit of Miami Beach. We bought an art deco house a few blocks from the mansion on North Bay Road, in a cheaper but attractive neighborhood. Our imagined resolution between North Bay Road and our frustrated back-to-the-land impulse was to live simply in our new premises but then to spend afternoons and weekends in the mansion swimming pool. That chance was lost when the owner, our friend who had presided over the mansion in its glorious epoch, moved to England. Her boyfriend, Bobby Gertz, the man with the beaded skullcap who presided over its entropy so brilliantly and for so long, had died earlier of a heart attack.

I could say that our lateral transfer was caused by weather, and to a certain extent that is true. The atmospheric pleasures of Florida were now a necessity with us. We thought about joining one of those rural communities of erudite New Englanders, or about settling in a northern college town for the sake of the children's education, but then when it came down to a choice between a fuller brain or warmer skin, we chose the skin. Winter we decided to avoid at all costs; sunshine was an irresistible asset for which we would give up all kinds of noble prospects. Loose clothes and bright skies were our determinants, and back on to Fisher's fully dredged habitat, we could have the sunshine without the mosquitoes that had made nature intolerable.

But that the visceral loyalty that recalled me to Florida in 1972 holds me permanently here now is an incomplete truth. More than the weather, I love the continuous rebellion, double-dealing, and crass maneuvering that Florida stimulates, and that my Pinkertonism abhors. At heart, I too am a rogue Floridian, and perhaps I could begin to come to terms with it, returning to Miami in the knowledge that the city as a whole was impossible to govern, and that a spectator who lingers is part of the spectacle.

We arrived in the area just in time to witness the results of the *Mariel* boatlift that Everglades fishermen had interrupted their marijuana smuggling to join. The Everglades, smouldering like peat in middrought, sent smoke over Miami on the days when the wind blew west, the city smelled like an all-alarm burn. The boatlift brought 100,000 new Cubans, young, poor, and raised on Castro, housed in tents around the Orange Bowl, covered by an immigrant status as flimsy and as hastily conceived as the tent city. The Carter administration was bested by south Florida's backyard navy, which had made and carried out its own foreign policy.

The president waffled; inviting the exodus one day, disinviting it the next. When his advisors informed him that Castro had sent his criminals and deranged to the boats, ridding himself of contract killers whose specialties were defined by the tattoos on the insides of their lips, the president ordered a halt to the flotilla. The boats kept coming and going, defying the Coast Guard, an agency that got as little respect now as when four of its agents were indicted for shooting a bootlegger. Thousands of Cubans a week were retrieved and dumped on the docks of Key West, then transported to Miami. The government could salvage only the illusion of control by creating a special category to approve the illegal entrants.

The deranged and the tattooed among them had no trouble finding Magnums, and in the dives and hangouts around their Orange Bowl tent city they began shooting each other. Every day was a story of twirling pistols and macho arguments, ending in corpses slumped over stools or on floors. At one grocery store five people were shot in a week. One Marielito killed another with a machine gun while both were driving separate cars and stopped at a stoplight; all over town, people decided never to complain at stoplights again. Marielitos contributed one-third of the Miami murders in six months: the killer imports plus the usual amount of domestic violence plus the cocaine cowboys brought the murder rate to a high-water mark. Bodies were left in trash bags, inside grocery carts dumped at the bottom of canals, in cleaning machines, under rug padding, in trunks. The morgue rented a refrigerated truck to handle the overload.

The Haitians were coming in, too, more victimized than victimizers, bewildered and malnourished, washed up like fruit on the beach. One of their boats was scuttled behind the Fontainebleau Hotel, a wreck among the little $5-an-hour sailing surfboards and it looked no more seaworthy, abandoned by people who ran down the beach and into town. Haitians who got caught by immigration were sent to the barbed-wire camps, but the camps held only a minority and decency demanded their release. In its own frustration at its lack of control, the Immigration Service went as mad as the rest of the town, taking a busload of Haitians detained in one of the camps and dumping them downtown at a shopping center in the middle of the night.

In the end, the government acquiesced to the *Mariel* boatlift because it feared that Miami's Cubans would riot if the boats were turned back, a kind of insecure calculation never applied to Little Rock or Selma during the Civil Rights struggles. Washington had patronized Miami as it might patronize a small but defiant Third World republic.

Miami rioted anyway, not the Cubans, but the blacks, tense and bitter at the hegemony of Cubans around them, more resentful of the Cubans, I think, than of the white Anglos. White, Anglo, Latin, non-Latin, black, Hispanic, that is what the town had come to.

The first black school superintendent in Dade County diverted school funds for his own gold plumbing fixtures, he was quickly convicted; a black insurance salesman, riding his motorcyle home from work, was bludgeoned to death and white policemen were acquitted. The logic of these two cases sent blacks out into the streets, the smoke from burning buildings mingling with the smoke from the fires in the Everglades, dead rioters occupying slabs next to dead Marielitos down at the refrigerated, add-on morgue.

In this chaos, we went about our business. Our neighborhood was calm, but we saw the smoke from Miami and the beached boats behind the Fontainebleau, and followed the riots and the mayhem in the newspapers. Newspapers are our social landscape, they emanated a foreboding. People formed crime-watch organizations, bought guns and practiced at rifle ranges; guns were little metal souvenirs of the events that authorities were powerless to control. There was so much foreboding in the *Miami Herald* that its editors wrote columns about Cubans who stopped to help Anglos change a tire, or about Anglos who rescued Cuban cats from trees, the daily pleasantries elevated to remarkable and commendable acts.

Parts of Miami had always been Cuban, but now you couldn't place an order in English at the Miami Beach Woolworth's and expect always to be understood. Although ours was a generally happy coexistence—strengthened in daily pleasantries, joint business ventures and mutual assistance on streets, at outdoor cafés, and in restaurants—Cubans were a constant source of consternation for the gringos in the area. Whether they got as wrought up about us I don't know.

The 100,000 Marielito Cubans brought the Spanish-speakers to a majority in the city of Miami, 80 percent of the population of Hialeah, and 75 percent of Sweetwater. Counting all the Cubans, Nicaraguans, Salvadorans, Peruvians, Panamanians, Colombians, and Argentinians, the Latins comprised a third of the county's residents; or, as a Cuban friend of mine said, "We thought we would retake Cuba but we are taking Dade County, instead." Exiles and immigrants expand their territory with the success of Cuban lizards, while the native xenophobes try futilely to hold them back with anti-bilingual laws, prohibiting official publications in Spanish. In an extraordinary denial of reality that shows the dissension under which this region operates, the new county Metrorail system, which will serve millions of Spanish-speaking tourists and residents, is forced by law to display direction signs and routing information only in English. It is the county's way of telling Latin America to get lost.

On the one hand, the Cubans have been in Miami long enough to have produced a second generation, long enough to have become Americanized. Young Cubans are bilingual and U.S.-educated; they have no memory of the island to which their parents have tried so desperately to return. Twenty-five years have moderated the desire of the first generation to retake the homeland. A quarter century they have been expecting it, enough time for middle-aged members of the Batista government to grow old, for young soldiers at the Bay of Pigs to become middle-aged. Wives of Batista senators play cards in their apartment houses and reminisce like Russian archduchesses in the tea rooms of Paris. When a Batista son, now a male model in Ft. Lauderdale, contemplates in the *Miami Herald* the restoration of the Batista monarchy through his own photogenic self, his commitment is taken as comedy.

There is still a remarkable organization called the Municipios, in which exiles from each of two hundred Cuban cities and towns meet, elect mayors, provincial governors, prefects, and even a vestigial Cuban president. Edgardo Caturlo, a Cuban in his sixties, was president of the Municipios in the last term. He was a lawyer in Cuba but couldn't practice here. With typical Cuban aplomb he studied for a teaching degree, ran a grocery store, and put three sons through U.S. law schools, all the while thinking he was going back to Cuba. Now, he has come to terms with burial in the U.S. "If you had told me ten years ago that I would never go back, I would have said you were crazy," Caturlo says. "But not now."

But in spite of the assimilation of Cubans, Miami seems more Latin Americanized than it did a decade earlier. The Latinization of Miami is diffuse, limitless, all-encompassing. It surrounds the gringo rather than the reverse, making the gringo feel like the alien—not in one street or district or barrio, but everywhere. Grocery store aisles are filled with odd vegetables, yams that look like driftwood, guanabana paste, strange melons, and the candles for spell-making and miracle-granting; and Miami politicians seek political support from the practitioners of Cuban voodoo. On the streets, Spanish is the official language. On street corners and in department stores, gringos are constantly addressed in the foreign tongue. We are not asked, "Do you speak Spanish?" which at least suggests the possibility that somebody might not speak it; we are assaulted in a barrage of Spanish words, delivered with the confidence that any Miami listener obviously would understand them. I can imagine how difficult it must be for the gringo monolingual; I speak the language, and yet sometimes I am so exasperated by the presumption that if somebody asks me, "Dónde está el ascensor," I answer, "What? What? No Speka Spanitch."

Miami is still a bivouac, a government-in-exile, not only for the Cubans but also for Nicaraguans and Haitians, Salvadorans and Hondurans who have taken up where the Cubans left off. It is not twenty-five years for all of them, their hopes for restoration are still fresh. Exiles from the poor end of Latin America coexist here with an incredible constellation of the deposed: the sons, wives, brothers, and mistresses of the Nicaraguan Somozas; relatives of the Trujillos; members of El Salvador's fourteen families; Panamanian presidents; the ex-mayor of Managua; various relatives of Haiti's President Jean Claude (Bébé Doc) Duvalier who have fallen into disfavor; members of the Somoza cabinet selling hot dogs and pencils; Peruvian and Bolivian generals.

At least twenty Nicaraguan generals and colonels and five hundred members of Somoza's national guard live in Miami, many in the trailer community of Sweetwater, working as parking lot attendants, car hops, security men. General Gonzalo Everts, hero of the battle of León, drives every night from his trailer home in Sweetwater to a construction site in south Dade, where he sits up all night watching for burglars, as he once watched for rebel troops in the Nicaraguan foothills. The Somoza army could be gathered up from the parking lots of Miami banks and department stores.

Haitians subsist as day laborers and maids, tuned into rogue radio stations that echo their expectations with fanciful reports of Bébé Doc's fatal disease and accidents (he fell off a horse, he was wounded by an arrow, he got syphilis). Haitians have marched in Miami living rooms to martial music, practicing rifle maneuvers with brooms supplied by would-be liberators. The most recent liberator, a Ft. Lauderdale gas station owner named Bernard Sansaricq, enlisted thirty or so Haitians from the department store security forces, armed and trained them, and on the illusion of his CIA support and his battalion in the Haitian foothills, these men allowed themselves to be flown to a Caribbean staging area, and five were sent on to Haiti, where they were captured and killed.

Sansaricq stayed behind to announce his victory to the radio, and he and the rest of the men floated prudently offshore in a small boat until they were picked up by the Coast Guard. The *Miami Herald*, unsure which local armies might be serious and which are ridiculous, gave Sansaricq's attack a front-page banner headline.

Many of Miami's recent arrivals drift in documentary ether, neither here nor there. Ninety percent of the Nicaraguans have been rejected in their requests for asylum, or else their cases are yet to be heard, and they and thousands of Haitians and other entrants live with the thought that they might be deported, which inhibits them from getting permanent jobs, getting degrees, learning English, and settling down.

This sort of half-adoption of Miami also applies to the wealthier immigrants, who have not given up their farms, businesses, political aspirations back home. Miami is a fail safe for the comfortable as much as it is a new start for the desperate; and that fact alone distinguishes its immigration from others in American history. Half the city's interests are here and half are there—back and forth through the airport go the money, the contracts, the agreements, the votes, the spies, the operatives, the oligarchs that operate in both realms.

Political and economic fortunes in each realm are tied to the other, the sale and resale of Miami condominiums depends on the exchange rates, the currency restrictions, and the street price of cocaine, as it fluctuates on confiscations. The occupancy of condominiums depends, in some cases, on who is in power where; during a recent campaign for the presidency of Colombia, candidates came to Miami to seek votes, because the most influential Colombians pull strings from Florida. Members of El Salvador's richest families pull strings from the high-rises on Brickell Avenue. Miami is a platform for the string-pullers of all the puppet governments from the continent below. Its banks are the repositories of national treasuries. It is to Miami that all the consequences of our support of tyrants and autocrats come back.

The city has absorbed too much vengeance to be lighthearted. Its politics are fanatical, as fanatical as when the Cubans launched their first anti-Castro raids. The middle-of-the-road local viewpoint on foreign affairs would be off-the-curb in Pittsburgh or Washington. A flip of the dial to Cuban radio takes the gringo into an antiworld where the right-wing armies of Chile and El Salvador are always "heroic" and their left-wing or moderate opponents are "cowards"; and this on the regular newscasts. The perception among first-generation exiles is that the *Miami Herald,* the city's moderate newspaper, is pro-Communist. The *Herald* has never said anything gratuitously flattering about Fidel Castro, but it has been thought to be soft on the enemy because is occasionally reports that even Castro has schools and hospitals. This objective style of American journalism is not understood by large potential segments of the Miami readership, who regard balanced coverage as a kind of literary treason.

Communism is the most important local issue in Miami, supplanting roads, garbage, and hospitals. One's stand on the great events in Central America is more important to one's political fate than one's stand on the city budget or its taxes. The journalist Hilda Inclan, who once shared our breakfast with Morales, recently reviewed a sixteen-month period during which the Miami City Commission passed numerous foreign-policy resolutions: declaring March 25 to be an official day for Orlando Bosch, the terrorist pediatrician; warning of an influx of Cuban spies into the city; condemning Universal Pictures for portraying a Cuban as a cocaine dealer in *Scarface;* urging the local convention center to refuse to admit any group from a Communist country; awarding city funds to a paramilitary alliance for a breakfast program; threatening to block a conference on the Caribbean because a socialist prime minister of Jamaica was invited to attend.

Mayor Maurice Ferre took a stand on human rights in Latin America at the Venezuelan bedside of Bosch the bomber, who was exonerated of the charge that he blew up the Cuban airliner but still was not released. How else could Mayor Ferre lead a city that mourned the death of Somoza, a city where a major television station put on a telethon for Cubans arrested for murdering the Chilean ambassador in Washington, a city that answers the shooting down of a Korean airliner with the burning of Russian flags, while it venerates the men suspected of having destroyed the Cuban plane?

The small-minded gringo carping, "Why don't they speak English?" comes from a deeper bewilderment at all the entangling alliances that Miami has formed. What confusions and suspicions its brand of internationalism has produced, first with its own navy and then with its own foreign policy. Does the administration neglect to investigate certain crimes here because it needs the support of oligarchs-in-hiding to carry on the Caribbean wars? An Argentine doctor, who was also an ex-ambassador, owned an abortion clinic on Biscayne Boulevard where four women died; the state charged him with several counts of unlawful practice of medicine and with manslaughter. The manslaughter charge was dismissed for lack of speedy prosecution and then restored on appeal; the ambassador, meanwhile, was convicted on one count of unlawful practice of medicine and then left town for Argentina. His lawyer says he is merely awaiting further developments, the state's attorney says he has fled justice. Is there an

Argentine diplomatic complication here, or simply another example of plodding due process? Such are the daily conundrums of journalists—forever unresolved.

And nowhere was uncertainty more pronounced than in the affairs of my old nemesis, Ricardo Morales, the greatest manipulator of them all.

Back to Business

The last time I had seen Morales was at that breakfast in Caracas. A rumor among journalists that he had been killed and deposited at the bottom of the Atlantic proved false: in 1978, while we still lived in Everglades City, he resurfaced in the *Miami Herald*. The headline read: "Cops Spy Familiar Face in Drug Bust."

Morales was pulled over while leading a procession of 5,000 pounds of marijuana. If he hadn't been attached to them, 5,000 pounds would not have been worth a story, for by the new Florida energy calculation, 5,000 pounds represented only seven barrels of oil. Our Venezuela nemesis was a Miami celebrity, famous less for his bombings and his rumored murders than for his stories. His lips had been on the ears of every spies' bureaucracy from Washington to Israel. Before and beyond our trivial encounter with him, he was called in front of grand juries investigating everything from the bathroom bombings at the Miami justice building to the assassination of President Kennedy.

He was Miami's premier informant, who, with Richelieu's guile, had managed to survive via partial cooperation with all sides, making himself unreliable but indispensable. No wonder he could lie to us without flinching. Those prosecutors we saw on the plane to Caracas had come to enlist Morales as their star witness in a Florida trial against a Cuban bomber; Morales agreed to testify, but didn't show up; he was still friendly with both the bomber and the prosecutors. When Morales was arrested for the marijuana, police found his concealed weapon in the car's glove compartment, his membership card from the Venezuelan secret police, plus a list of confidential radio frequencies from the Drug Enforcement Administration, the Coast Guard, the FBI, the Secret Service, the Florida Highway Parol, and the Miami and Miami Shores police departments.

Drugs again: is that where everything coalesces in this nebulae of casinos, armies, intriguers, bombers, the mob, and the CIA? It began to seem as if fishing, spying, everything reduced to bales. I wouldn't have expected it of Morales after my brief encounter with him; he seemed too obsessed with anticommunism, and courier for a small truckload was too plebeian a role for such a man. But apparently, he had returned from Venezuela in 1976 to turn his back on his old anti-Castro colleagues. His most visible new friend was Carlos Quesada, an apolitical Cuban who, during all those years the patriotic exiles had devoted themselves to routing Castro, was more devoted to things like breaking into cars. Quesada was a sharp dresser, but Italian suits and lizard shoes did not make him the equal of Ricardo Morales.

The two of them hung around the Mutiny Club in Miami's Coconut Grove. The Mutiny Club was a representative high-roller bar, it cost $75 for an exclusive membership and the $75 was the only exclusivity required. The place was decorated with potted palms and elephant ears, making the room look like a Rousseau, the waitresses wore leotards and colorful hats, appearing to be the animals of paradise. Their patrons included the cocaine dealers of Miami and Coconut

Grove, plus half the investigative agents in the various local police departments, sitting at opposite positions, hiding behind the foliage, making calls back to their respective headquarters from the phones at every table.

It was in this setting, so spiritually removed from the little coffee shops of Southwest Eighth Street, from the urgency and desperation that drove Cuban men to spend half their nights out on the open sea, making pinprick raids at the Castro coast, that Morales conspired with his lesser associate. Sometimes they met at the Mutiny; other times they met at Quesada's little house, one of those Miami dwellings with metal grilles on the windows and a speedboat parked out front, and with a security system worth more than the real estate. There was Morales, there was Quesada, there were several other Cubans with prior arrest records; together they conspired to distribute, separately they informed on each other to members of various police agencies who could be seen at the Mutiny, between the leaves.

The drug smuggling business in Miami demanded the same skills as the spying business. A smuggler couldn't survive by keeping quiet, because too many people were talking about him. He needed a police agency to which he could inform on others, or at least an agent or two who would return the favor by keeping him up-to-date on who was trying to bust him. A silent smuggler had nothing with which to bargain, and neither did a silent police department, and so each side constantly dropped hints: the major targets of one agency were undoubtedly the key informants for the next. When someone was busted in Miami, it usually meant that his value as a storyteller was exceeded by his value as an arrest statistic.

Carlos Quesada, Morales's new friend, must have been a deficient storyteller, because two other partners in his business had informed on him and he didn't know it. Their accusations were used as the basis for a wiretap application on

Quesada's phone. For six months the phone was tapped and Quesada was unaware of that, too. In March, 1978, police arrested Quesada and eight associates and seized $913,000 and fifty-six pounds of cocaine. Morales must have known something: he wasn't picked up.

It was a subsequent marijuana delivery, arranged two weeks later on Quesada's phone, apparently on the assumption that the tap was off, that resulted in Morales's capture. From the disadvantaged position of being handcuffed and dragged off to jail, Morales began his conquest of the Miami legal system.

First he was acquitted, but acquittal is not spectacular in this town; Morales had good lawyers, he got the two informers to forget their earlier testimony, and so the wiretaps based on their stories were thrown out of court. Morales never took the stand, but somehow his presence was so commanding that the state attorney who lost the case and had a heart attack would later say he respected and admired the defendant as much as any man he had met.

The law was through with Morales, but not the reverse: when the trial of his friend Quesada and the eight associates convened, Ricardo was sitting in the audience. He and the prosecutor in this case, a federal case, recognized each other immediately. It was Jerry Sanford, assistant U.S. attorney in Miami, who had been wrapped up in bombing cases and political murders in which suspects were CIA-trained exiles, and now his big cases were drug cases involving some of the same people as before, and the results were no better. Morales would have recognized any number of federal prosecutors, he had had so many dealings with them, going back to his testifying against the terrorist pediatrician. Jerry Sanford had been the prosecutor at one of the bombing trails where Morales was billed as star witness but failed to appear.

Sanford had no apparent reason to trust Ricardo Morales,

and yet he not only trusted him, he said he loved him. Morales fever was a Miami epidemic, Sanford had an extreme case of it, so did the prosecutor in the marijuana trial, policemen, drug dealers, CIA agents, lawyers, and journalists expelled from Venezuela. All described him as charming and charismatic, and after he undercut them and deceived them, still they believed in him.

It was the subversive Miami context that Morales worked to his benefit, in the substratum of mutual suspicion, where doubts about the appearance of things harmonized with the false passports and multiple identities, there was always some level on which Morales could claim that his double-cross was in the ultimate best interest of the victim. He did it to us in Venezuela; he did it twice to the terrorist pediatrician, who, I found out later, had been lured to Caracas and jailed on Morales's orders; he did it to prosecutors and attorneys.

When Sanford and Morales met in the hallway of the courtroom at the Quesada drug trial, Morales had a proposal to advance. Would the U.S. government be willing to dismiss charges against Carlos Quesada in return for Quesada's cooperation in the prosecution of the balance of the defendants? The way Morales presented it, his plan would benefit both his friend Quesada, whose freedom would be assured, and his friend Sanford, who might need Quesada's help to gain some convictions, which in Miami was difficult.

Even the judge was astounded when the assistant U.S. attorney, speaking for the prosecution, announced that Carlos Quesada had been granted immunity and would now appear as a government witness against mostly lesser defendants. Sanford was gratified, he was now certain to win the case. Quesada was gratified, not only had Morales gotten him out of trouble, Morales also had unburdened Quesada of some of the guilt of ratting on his friends by having Quesada's car shot full of machine-gun bullets so it looked as if Quesada was only retaliating for what the others had done to him. Machine-gun bursts are gross music, but with Morales, they were an accompaniment to a very subtle orchestration.

Morales was especially gratified. He wasn't a lawyer, wasn't even a U.S. citizen, and yet an episode that began with his own embarrassing arrest ended with the prosecution taking his advice. The next time Carlos Quesada needed legal help, Morales suggested Jerry Sanford, now gone into private practice, so the prosecutor became Quesada's lawyer. The police department that had spent nine hundred hours monitoring Quesada's phone calls and trying to put him in jail now had to assign him a police bodyguard, as protection against possible harm from the other eight men he had helped convict. So Quesada's captors became Quesada's guardians. By the force of Morales's singular and subversive influence, the people who arrested Quesada were now shielding him, the prosecutor was now defending him, and Quesada's other eight partners, Morales's erstwhile competitors, were removed to the penitentiary so that the two Cubans, one CIA-trained, the other apolitical, could get back to business.

In December, 1981, roughly a year after our return to Miami Beach, the informant sat with two policemen in the parking lot of Monty Trainer's dockside bar in Coconut Grove. Patrons drank oversized rum punches, absorbed the music of a steel band, contemplated the masts of moored sailboats, and convinced themselves they would prefer to be drifting on the Gulf Stream. Morales had chosen this spot to tell the police that Carlos Quesada, his old friend, was a drug dealer.

The police already knew Quesada was a drug dealer, one of them was a bodyguard assigned by the court to protect Quesada from physical harm after his flip in the last trial.

How could they resist laughing when the author of the Quesada Compromise advised them, as a concerned non-citizen, that Quesada should be investigated anew.

Nevertheless, the justice system listened to Morales and a state's attorney took his deposition at the Holiday Inn. Morales, who scared off the informants for the last wiretap, had become the crucial informant for a new one, his deposition being the basis for a formal application for a bug in Quesada's phone and a bug in the wall clock. Police called the case Operation Tick-Talks, to distinguish it from a humdrum drug bust. The clock would be ticking while Quesada and company were talking.

Given his history of buzzing in all ears, of flitting and feinting around various courtrooms, would the state of Florida ally itself with Morales once again? Its wariness of this mercurial collaborator was overcome by the irresistible prospect that he dangled in front of it. Numerous well-publicized cases had been confused by CIA connections, by interlocking directorates of informants; to win one, you needed a Morales on your side. This time, he said he could deliver Quesada and more than Quesada, he could deliver a virtual brigade from the Bay of Pigs. It would be a reunion of sorts, a glorious recap of twenty years of Miami achievement, a reunion in handcuffs.

Morales drew them all in at the Mutiny Bar. The late night celebrations at his table there in the last months of 1981 joined CIA agents with local police, bombers with prosecutors, smugglers with journalists. It was a clandestine operator's "This Is Your Life."

Rafael Villaverde was there; this oversized and ebullient Cuban, a veteran of the Bay of Pigs, was a prominent Miami success story. Villaverde was arrested on the Cuban beach in 1961, jailed by Castro and then ransomed by President Kennedy for medicine and car parts, returned to Miami to pick tomatoes in the migrant fields, advanced to the directorship of a $2-million-a-year antipoverty agency for the Latin elderly, an agency periodically investigated as a meeting place for terrorists. Villaverde admitted that so-called terrorists visited his agency. He said they were evaluating the social services that they someday would require. Negative publicity in the gringo media was still good publicity among the Cubans: Villaverde was most respected for the fact that he was still freelance CIA, invited to take off to South America and Europe to assassinate important leftists. In Miami, welfare directors can moonlight as contract hit men.

Jerry Sanford, the Quesada prosecutor cum Quesada lawyer, also visited Morales's table. Raúl Díaz was there; Díaz was the son-in-law of Watergate soldier Rolando Martínez and also one of the policemen who shared our flight to Venezuela. Díaz represented local law enforcement. Carlos Quesada was there, representing the drug faction, his lowlier associates removed to jail, now Morales had up-leveled him with these important new friends.

All of the phases of Morales's life were united in his company; all the representatives had reasons to distrust the informer but could not resist him; some, like the drug dealers and the police, were official antagonists brought together by the essential unreliability of their host, who was loyal enough to hold supporters from one camp, never loyal enough to lose them from another.

By night, Morales entertained the entire group with clever jokes and stories. By day, he sold out one faction to the other, telling the state prosecutors and the police that he could give them Villaverde, he could give them Villaverde's brother Raúl, he could give them the unfortunately named Condom brothers, also veterans of the Bay of Pigs, he could give them Frank Castro, likewise a victim of an unfortunate name, but who made up for it in dedication to the destruction of his bearded namesake. One person Morales couldn't give them was Orlando Bosch, the terrorist pediatrician, but that was only because Bosch was still in jail. Morales had already given him to the Venezuelans.

His motive in reuniting these patriotic Cubans and then informing on them for drug smuggling was the object of many discussions among police and prosecutors who knew of the meeting in the police car at Monty Trainer's parking lot. Morales himself told police it was because he drew the line at heroin: "Heroin . . . goes against, you know, my own belief and religion, and you know I . . . flatly refuse to go along in this new kind of business," but nobody could believe that the Cubans were smuggling heroin, or that Morales's religion was based on a moral distinction between the various controlled substances.

Simple assumptions led to the usual boggle of speculations. Morales's actions were as imponderable to Miami police and attorneys as they had been to us the day he kicked us out of Venezuela. One theory was that he was feuding with Carlos Quesada and had decided to turn Quesada in, that the Bay of Pigs veterans were incidental. Another theory was that Morales had been feuding with Rafael Villaverde, his old CIA comrade-in-arms, and that Quesada was incidental. The Villaverde theory gained support one night at the Mutiny Bar, when Morales and the welfare director had a nasty debate about spy matters and Morales supported his position with little pats of butter, launched against Villaverde's dress shirt.

Who ever understood why these people did things? The state of Florida acted on straight-line gringo assumptions, Morales on its side, Morales against the drug dealers. Quesada's phone was retapped, police sent on surveillance missions to the very site they surveilled before, and Morales disappeared into a witness protection program. In 1982, Tick-Talks made headlines: forty-eight people arrested in a city-wide roundup, including Villaverde the anti-poverty director, his brother Raúl, the Condom brothers, Frank Castro the anti-Castro paratrooper, schoolteachers, accountants, and Carlos Quesada.

In the period between the arrests and the trial I became a Morales watcher, amazed and amused. His erstwhile comeuppance, state of Florida versus Morales, had resulted in the reputation of the state attorney's office resting on his word. Perhaps I wouldn't have been so amused had I not just come from Everglades City where law and order were civic myths, and I was better prepared to consider Morales with some detachment.

I was in the courtroom during the pretrial hearing on whether the Tick-Talks conversations would be admitted as evidence. The transcripts were stacked up like telephone books in the halls and between the desks over at the state's attorney's office, waiting for the judge's ruling. Veterans of the Bay of Pigs, now the defendants of Tick-Talks, sat in the judicial pews while their lawyers, some of the best in Miami, argued that the wiretaps should be banished from the case. Quesada the drug dealer was in the courtroom, wearing conservative brown suits and looking generally somber; Frank Castro was there, short and muscular like a jockey; Rafael Villaverde was absent, having disappeared in a strange offshore boating accident in which six survivors said he had died, yet there was gossip of an arranged disappearance.

The pretrial hearing was another Morales reunion, without the principal, but he monopolized it in absentia. For two weeks, his history and psychology were debated and analyzed by a procession of witnesses. The case depended on the wiretaps, the wiretaps depended on the reliability of the informant.

Rina Cohan, young state's attorney, tried to build Morales up; Morales, meanwhile, was dialing up every reporter he knew, trying to make himself sound as unreliable as possible.

He confessed to murders, to Miami bombings, to almost every crime that he was ever called to help solve. It was devastating self-incrimination, Morales called the *Herald,* he called me, his big scoop was about the bombing of the airliner for which the terrorist pediatrician still sat in a Caracas jail. "You know who did that?" Morales asked. "I did it. I killed those people. I am the bomber."

For several days in a row, the state of Florida struggled to defend Morales against his own evidence, planted in the morning editions. What absurd theater it was. To support Morales and save the wiretaps, a Miami policeman testified under oath that blowing up a Cuban airliner was not such a bad thing to do.

The state's attorney announced that she would put Ricardo Morales on the stand, if only to prove that he existed. After all the fantastic testimony, the judge began to look as if he doubted it. Morales in person: for at least a week the courtroom worked itself up to his appearance. Bay of Pigs veterans were in more frequent attendance, damning Morales in the hallways.

The courtroom was cleared, and the bailiffs installed a walk-through metal detector, the kind used at airports. The machine told us all who would be the next witness.

He came through the side door to the left of the judge's bench. His loose-fitting velour shirt covered a bigger stomach than the stomach I saw in the hotel room in Caracas, his glasses hung from a V-neck shirt, he wore designer jeans. Morales's entrance was a letdown only relative to the visions that he catalyzed.

He approached the wooden rail separating him from me and from the old friends he betrayed in Tick-Talks: Quesada, Frank Castro, Raúl Villaverde, brother of the Villaverde who disappeared in the sea. The double-crosser confronted his current victims, brought himself to attention, and saluted.

The victims stiffened and returned the salute, twenty years of anti-Castro heroics were caught up in that gesture. A salute from the Bay of Pigs; Cubans were still united in that cause, with the movement of one hand Morales swept away all their anger, the betrayer and the betrayed were returned to being soldiers, soldiers against Communism, everything that might divide them at that moment, trivialized. Morales, Frank Castro, Villaverde, embraced across the railing like lost friends, hugging and patting each other on the back. The prosecutor, Rina Cohan, made an effort to appear impassive, but any doubt about the future of Tick-Talks was now removed; we all knew the Tick-Talks case was over.

It made no sense for the state to rely on him now. Morales took the stand, but the prosecutor had no questions. "No questions?" the judge asked, incredulous. "So why do we need Mr. Morales?"

"If the state has no questions, the court has no questions, the defense has no questions, therefore, Mr. Morales is excused." A few weeks later, the judge ruled against the wiretaps, charges were dropped, prosecutors and police had to apologize for hundreds of wasted hours in taping and deciphering, unfortunately, they had chosen an unreliable informant.

The Florida legal system was no better match for Ricardo Morales than I was, it fell to his CIA training and his practiced subversions. There was more gossip in the Cuban coffee shop that Tick-Talks may have been a drug case for the gringos, but for the Cubans it had never been a drug case, from the beginning they had seen it as an extension of the spies' squabble between Morales and Rafael Villaverde, the antipoverty director lost in the ocean. Maybe Morales and Villaverde were in subterranean cahoots; forty-eight people arrested just so Villaverde could have a good excuse for disappearing, before he thought of a better excuse with the boat accident; Morales fixing it so none of the forty-eight would be convicted. Some speculated that the Miami antipoverty director was on a secret CIA mission in Nicaragua.

Morales left town, I think. Then, later in 1982, he resurfaced in his last *Miami News* headline: "Morales Shot on Key Biscayne." He had taken a woman friend to a bar at the Rogers-on-the-Green restaurant. There was an argument; Morales defended the woman's right to take her drink outside in a regular glass instead of a plastic cup. Morales reached for the gun in his sock, apparently an employee fired his, witnesses scattered, there were no charges filed. Morales died the next day. Survivor of the secret war, double-crosser of terrorists, informer on drug dealers, expert in plastique and the recoilless rifle—killed for plastic take-out.

In an unexpected fit of sentiment, I wanted to send flowers. The hospital gave me the name of the funeral home, but the funeral home denied there was a body.

The Great America Trading Company

Bobby Gertz, guru of my reentry, the brilliant impersonator, the man who said "Eat now, you'll eat later," and imported straw hats or something else, was the perfect Florida master. The mansion on North Bay Road, which I had thought so aberrant, was a perfect cell of Florida substance, with its poolside diversions, its retiree subsidy, its clandestine occupations, its lot dredged by Fisher, its open-door policy, and its generous indifference to the quality of resident.

Miami is clarified as a city of a thousand fronts. Its developers did not plan it that way, certainly not the sober Henry Flagler, and yet one cannot view its adoption of four secret enterprises—Prohibition, gambling, drug smuggling, and the Cuban war—as gratuitous fortune, nor can one credit only the Latin Americans. Perhaps in the artificial origins, the fantasy architecture, the illusions of promoters is the source of a familiarity for appearance that makes southern Florida so receptive to undercover work.

So much of what we touch and see continues to have subterranean implications. There was the salvage for our Everglades house, belonging to the dictator and the ex-Mafioso;

the grocery store where we buy French cheese, once bombed by Ricardo Morales, who mistook it for a bookie joint next door; the owner of the garage where I get my car fixed, the subject of a federal narcotics investigation and linked to the CIA; and a bigger house on which we once made an offer, owned by an ex-mob boss from Chicago and, locally, the king of the pinball machines.

The great percentage of south Floridians live a law-abiding normalcy, pay their taxes, worry about overdue parking tickets, and wonder if behind and around them is not the outlaw capital of the world. One searches for comparisons in North Africa, the Bahamas, San Francisco in the Gold Rush, perhaps? What would Lincoln Steffens have said about Miami, Steffens the muckraker from the early 1900s, who found that "St. Louis exemplified boodle; Minnesota, police graft; Pittsburgh, a political and industrial machine; and Philadelphia, general civic corruption." That Miami is all sunshine and shady deals?

Once, Bobby Gertz turned the mansion on North Bay Road into the Great America Trading Company. He purchased ledger books and put price tags on all the bizarre items from South America. The purpose of this elaborate caper was to satisfy a probation officer that one of the residents, who had been busted with cocaine in his glove compartment, had a job: clerk of Great America. Is Miami a city with cocaine in its glove compartment, pretending to be the Great America Trading Company? It is headquarters for Eastern Airlines and Burger King, shipping companies and light industry and so forth, and yet whether the legitimate revenues exceed the illegitimate cash flow is the crucial, and therefore, the unanswered question.

Prosperity is obvious in the Mercedeses on the roads, the stores that sell $100 shirts, the high-rise office buildings that sprout up on Brickell Avenue like concrete bamboo along the waddies of the bay, each outshooting the next, all requiring variances and exemptions so that the Miami on the books could never be mistaken for this wild and in some ways beautiful satire on zoning.

Half of the rich people seem to be in real estate and the other half have undisclosed sources of revenue; half of the fanciest buildings seem to be hotels or condos and the other half banks. Both halves do a big cash business. The federal reserves for this district are still awash in cash, cash from the drug business that may have disappeared from the front pages but not from economic life, cash that avoids confiscatory regimes, cash that avoids credit restrictions, cash that avoids taxes, illegal cash looking for legal havens, or legal cash looking for illegal havens, cash that is laundered, and cash that needs laundering, drug cash, mob cash, mixed with flight capital, cash joined in the great eddy of clean and dirty enterprises, producing the brackish flow on which this city is sustained.

Real estate agents, car dealers, lawyers, yacht brokers, and jewelers are our Steffenses; they have seen the briefcases full of bills that buy their services. I met a real estate agent who relocates oligarchs; she is the person to call in Miami if a government is about to fall. She has sold to Colombians, Venezuelans, and Peruvians, some who get their dollars out through banks, others who simply send cash in the mails and hope that half will arrive, trading in condos as speculation or as security. Colombians, she says, are like turtles, slow and methodical buyers; Venezuelans, more volatile and impulsive; she knows of entire development projects that sell out to one nationality or another.

Charles Kimball is a real estate analyst who keeps track in a more scientific way; every time a building or a piece of land worth more than $300,000 is purchased in the Miami or Ft. Lauderdale area, he writes the names of buyers and sellers on a three-by-five card.

During a recent two-year period, and before the Latin American economies went bad, 30 percent of this expensive real estate was bought up by offshore corporations formed to hide the identities of the buyers. High-rises, industrial parks, commercial districts acquired by unnamed parties, is this what Adam Smith meant by the Invisible Hand? Never give your right name, even to a Sears deliveryman, Gertz taught; south Florida is a material tribute to his lesson.

Manolo Reboso, the Cuban candidate for Miami mayor, had an interest in an offshore corporation, and after the *Miami Herald* asked some questions about what the newspaper believed were some $9 million funneled through it and unaccounted for, he withdrew from the race, has kept a low profile since, and has not been charged with anything. President Nixon's house on Key Biscayne was sold to an offshore corporation; the house was razed and a new one built on the property; the current occupant is a Colombian who objected to Channel 10's insinuations of hanky-panky and has sued the local TV station. He says he knows nothing about drug smuggling or money laundering, and that there is no link between him, his offshore corporation, and two Colombian brothers whose names came up in a Florida Department of Law Enforcement probe.

That the Florida jails are full one realistically understands, and yet from the general run of things, one wonders: filled by whom? Drugs cases with tradenames seem inevitably to end in the defendants either jumping bail or returning to Colombia or Bolivia, or else, if they are important enough, given immunity for informing on lesser associates. Ten years of the publicized war on drugs, culminating in the glut of cocaine, has left Miami with the impression that drug law enforcement is not a profession so much as a tax-supported compulsion.

Escape is the constant theme, one can almost catalogue the Miami escapes: million-dollar bond-out; case dismissed for lack of speedy prosecution; case dismissed from CIA complication; case dropped for diplomatic repercussion; case closed. Adventurers come here, spend money, strike a pose, get rich, get exposed, and then steal away, sometimes in a matter of months.

Sheik Mohammed Al-Fassi was the most sought-after man in Miami after his move here from Beverly Hills. He was not a real sheik, but who cared? At the Diplomat Hotel in Hollywood (Fla.) Al-Fassi still had enough clout to hold up all the elevators for several hours, according to newspaper reports, while his entourage checked out. For bodyguards, he hired 51 of the 98 police officers of Hallandale, and then 150 of the 290 officers of Hollywood, all the while building and renovating mansions through his offshore corporation, and setting up parades in his honor in small cities.

Al-Fassi's wife sued him for the custody of their children in the Miami courts, her attorney kept telling the judge that Al-Fassi would leave town with the children if he were not in some way detained. The judge said he could not imagine that such a thing would happen, until the day the sheik took off for Saudi Arabia like the Magic Moslem, leaving behind numerous claimants—including lawyers, craftsmen, hotel owners—who said the sheik owed them money. Real estate analyst Kimball told a congressional subcommittee that there are $5 million in unpaid claims against the Al-Fassi houses, and that money lost on the sheik's Star Island estate was part of the largest known fraud ever perpetrated in the U.S. by a Netherlands Antilles offshore corporation.

The next-celebrated escapee to Saudi Arabia was Alvin Malnik, owner of the Miami Beach Forge Restaurant, for years reputed to be the heir to the Meyer Lansky crime empire, and for years denying it. Malnik's car was bombed while he wasn't in it; some said it was a sign that his local services no longer would be required. Malnik is Jewish, but was last reported to be contemplating the wisdom of Mohammed.

In 1977, Albert Duque, a young Colombian, bought the house next to the mansion on North Bay Road. Whatever we thought about him, we were wrong, his success was not based on drugs. On a reputation for largess that comes with being a Colombian, and on a quiet and sympathetic demeanor, Duque acquired small coffee companies, two private jets, yachts; he took over the City National Bank of Miami in a stock transfer. He and his Colombian companies received $122 million in loans from more than twenty U.S. banks on bills of lading for coffee that the banks claim did not exist. At last notice, Duque was still sitting on North Bay Road, living off disbursements from the bankruptcy court, surrounded by creditors, awaiting the results of a criminal investigation, denying all charges, telling the newspapers that he is a recluse.

Every week, there is a story of delightful imposture that makes us forget the last. Most recently, two rather unlikely filmmakers brought cameras and a musical script to Miami Beach. They were praised in the press, flattered by priests, and, in a large public ceremony, awarded the keys to the city by the mayor himself. The adulation had hardly subsided before the two were dragged off by the FBI, the feds contending that the men were involved in a money-laundering scheme.

Our amazement at the local high achievers, at the uncanny procession of false prophets and sleazy risers, turns eventually into a groggy acceptance. What is extraordinary from an outsider's perspective is to us routine; yet all the signals and insinuations are abandoned as a path to a conclusion. Miami likens itself to a common metropolis with a common index of chicanery. More interesting, even, than the events described above is Miami's denial; the city is more upset at its image of wrongdoing than at the fact of it. Lately, the politicians are disturbed that a new television series might portray us, of all things, as crime-ridden. The mayor is concerned about the demoralizing effect of sex on cable channels. The city wonders if the viewers of the Miss Universe pageant, held in Miami, were left with a good impression. Out-of-town journalists who dwell on the obvious are dismissed as fictionalizers, just as they were in the Prohibition era.

South Florida is eternally stuck between the rogues who run things and the retirees and tourists who want to be reassured that they don't. On the highway, when there is a senior citizen driving an Oldsmobile at 10 miles per hour in front of me and a teenager driving a Mercedes at 75 behind, I know that I have settled into the Florida groove.

Roots in the Landfill

Who among us is rooted in Florida deep enough to complain of strangers in our midst? The Cubans seem to belong to Miami, at least they brought their children with them, at least they come from the subtropics. They are descendants of the Spaniards who cleared out in the eighteenth century, returned to repossess.

Gringos who complain about losing Miami to the aliens are aliens from an opposite direction. That great and uncompromising sweep of Spanish-speakers across Dade County is no different in essence than the sweep of midwesterners down the west coast from Clearwater to Naples into the layaway subdivisions and along the beaches of my childhood. There the smorgasbord eaters and protected-by-Pinkertons conquered all, crowding the restaurants, calling their motels Michiganer, Illinoiser, Indianan, their subdivisions Oakwood Estates, Fox Run, and the Heather, forcing the native strangers inland.

WASPs along the Gulf, Jews along the Atlantic, all migrated to Florida in discrete and impervious clusters, happy to be rid of the disturbing social mix of subspecies they left back north, compromising with their new location as little as possible.

Two decades, four decades, it is as if Florida has never touched them. In our new Miami Beach neighborhood, there are old people on the way down and young people on the way up, passing through or passing out, but not grounded here. The Cuban woman across the street has lived on Miami Beach for twenty years and she can't speak English, the Orthodox Jews next door practice self-denying rituals that contradict the spirit of hedonism that produced the first terry-cloth beach towel. Down the block and regardless of the season, we pass a parade of Lubavitchers wrapped in ankle-length blacks coats and topped in huge fur caps manufactured for Eastern European winters.

Among my contemporaries—the middle-aged professionals who find themselves working for the local newspapers, for a university, or for some other business that has brought them to Miami—the obsessive theme is when they will go back: back to Philadelphia, Washington, New England, California. Florida is beyond the familiar geography for them; at parties and in restaurants they name the stores on Madison Avenue or describe the current show at the Metropolitan or argue about whether Bloomingdale's is on Lexington and Sixty-third or Lexington and Fifty-ninth, and thereby stake their real claims.

The Cubans, ironically, may be the only aliens left who don't expect to go somewhere else someday. Susan has been living in Florida for twelve years since our meeting at the mansion and will always be a New Yorker. Our older children, both born in New York, spent seven years in Everglades City and now have spent three on Miami Beach, and they, too, think of themselves as transplanted easterners.

Florida is spiritually unclaimed. On this higher level, it does not seem to exist. There is no harmonic abstraction, no stereotype such as the cowboy, the Yankee trader, the trapper, the woodsman, the planter—no hero of history around which the population can rally. Perhaps it is the inevitable result of the invention of a past by the public relations departments. There is a certain culinary unity in stone crabs, but nothing like the populist glue of Boston baked beans, Baltimore soft-shells, or Texas chili. Texas has its ugly differences of opinion, but Texas has Tex-Mex; Florida has yet to develop a Flo-Cube.

There are writers of consequence in Florida, but are they Florida writers? Marjorie Kinnan Rawlings had her palmetto scrub culture; Hemingway had his Key West bar; Frank Conroy had his yo-yo; Tennessee Williams did lesser work here; John D. MacDonald wrote better books as a young novelist up North, before he moved to Florida and invented his beach bum, Travis McGee, who acts like a James Bond but thinks like a retiree; Harry Crews is in Gainesville putting snakes in discarded Deep South washing machines; Thomas McGuane got onto drugs and fish and began to sound like a Florida writer, then went off with his friends to become the Montana School of Writers because Florida is not a medium.

This is my context—St. Petersburg, Miami Beach—my roots are in the landfill. What serious and everlasting work a landfill could produce I do not know. Certainly, there is no Yoknapatawpha County under here, dig two feet and you hit water. On Carl Fisher's muckspit, I search my soul and draw a blank.

To walk the length of Miami Beach takes three hours. The beach itself, that is, that last remaining bit of natural geologic substance, the original sand of the barrier island, has recently been replaced by an artificial beach, dredged in by the Army Corps of Engineers. The beach disappeared, in part, because hotel owners tried to capture a relative advantage with groins, the groins hastened the erosion below, and, finally, with the Atlantic Ocean approaching the hotel back steps, engineers came to the rescue with the artificial beach, made so wide that it looks less like a seascape than like the oil fields near Bahrain.

Miami Beach is resolved, the man-made process complete. It is not a live beach; a shovel does not bring up the burrowing coquina shells. It is an industrial beach, industrial in grit and in concept, industrial and roomy.

There is the strip of beach, the strip of hotels, and then Collins Avenue, running north and south. All of the archaeology of Florida from the first scoops of Fisher onward are laid out here, as in a horizontal dig. I start at the north end, where high-priced condominium apartment buildings bracket the thoroughfare like sheer cliffs. This is the most expensive Miami Beach real estate, occupied by people who once came to the beach for a vacation, and then came back the next year and the year after that, moving from outdated hotels—that is, last season's hotels—into the newer hotels, and then into the hotels newer than that, and, finally, into the condos.

Recently, the condos have not been selling well. Many of them are vacant, the popularity of Miami Beach as a whole having declined, the action having moved to Boca Raton or Ft. Lauderdale. The Philadelphia builder whose daughter's trust fund financed our leisure at the mansion on North Bay Road still has a condo in the cavern, but he spends part of his time at Lake Tahoe, in Arizona, or in Southern California.

Below the condo cavern, there is the Fontainebleau and the Eden Roc, which along with the Doral and the Konover are among the few hotels still worthy of good reputation. The Fontainebleau is renovated, but it has not lost its effect. Its original architect, Morris Lapidus, seemed to have poured into it every outlandish ornament he could find, although it is less ornate than the simplest of Italian churches.

Outside the Fontainebleau, I see packs of old ladies with skin light yellow and ruddy, skin like faded rinds of grapefruit, painted up in heavy red rouge. They have outlived their husbands; the inevitable happens even on Miami Beach, which once prohibited cemeteries, and Miami Beach has passed St. Petersburg in average age of its inhabitants. I grew up with old people; I am comfortable among them now. Never does one feel younger than in the company of octogenarians, although I am nearly halfway to eighty myself, and no longer can I associate octogenarians with the arrival of the conquistadores.

There was a party, recently, to celebrate Miami Beach's sixty-fifth birthday. A contest was held for best cake. The cakes were all shaped like hotels, and the cake makers wore funny hats. I am reminded again how new Florida is, its most historic buildings still younger than its most historic inhabitants, that line of maturity when buildings predate old-timers is just now being passed.

Below the Fontainebleau and Eden Roc are the hotels from the Pink Cadillac period, the late 1940s and the early 1950s: San Souci, Versailles, Seville, Caribbean, Recency, Cadillac, Crown. They show signs of abandonment: chipped paint and boards on windows, rust stains from the old room air conditioners. Hotel rooms are being sold off as condos or with ninety-nine-year leases, or if not that, then the fate of these places is tied to cut-rate foreign group tours that depend on favorable exchange rates.

Smaller and smaller the hotels get as you walk south, with more and more sunshine, more and more openness, cheaper and cheaper rooms. We are thirty blocks below the condos now, back in the mid-1940s, where for $40 a night you can get a space on the same beach that costs $150 a night farther upland.

There is a man in blue shorts and matching terry cloth shirt, big belly, legs like tripod legs, rubber sandals. He is standing at the counter of a Cuban coffee shop, ordering bagels in English while blowing cigar smoke into the eggs of his countermates. He is Floridian in the absolute indifference to the spectacle he creates, his indomitable unawareness of the subtleties of language and customs, or of the effect of his paunch and his smoke on appetites. In California or New York, you must work on your body before you display it, Florida makes no such demands, this guy is rolling out of his elastic uninhibited, showing himself off with the aplomb of a torso builder.

Now we are in deli terrority, Wolfie's and the Concord cafeteria. Wolfie's isn't Wolfie's anymore, the waitresses are too polite. At the Concord, the French toast is as thick as a good dictionary and the big room in which it is eaten has the clientele of an off-track betting shop. Delis and porno movie houses, transistor and camera stores, beach sandals and plastic luggage, Cuban cafés—we are approaching Lincoln Road, once Fifth Avenue South, where you could buy the gold, the jade, the minks that were required subtropical leisurewear during the casino-nightclub phase. Lincoln Road is reduced to digital clocks, tennis shoes, alterationists, and the kind of cheap office space from which I write these words.

From here south there is no pretense to resort; this is a real city now, with urban masses and poverty, poverty right along the artificial beach. Below Lincoln Road are the kosher nursing homes and open fruit markets where old Jews stand in line to buy an orange or three apples and because of their budgets, haggle over change. Many live on social security, they share the neighborhood with the tattooed and cashless *Mariel* Cuban refugees, who because of the low rent, made Miami Beach their first U.S. address.

The elderly Jews sit on porches of two- and three-story rooming houses, arranged in rows like so many Yiddish-speaking birds lined up against a wind. Many have been here thirty years; many, I suspect, have never gone onto the beach.

What a wonderful joke on Carl Fisher. Of all the species he lured to his city, only Jews were not invited. His hotel managers took to nose-watching and reporting back the names of Jewish-sounding patrons so they could be politely asked to leave—all except wealthy Jews like Julius Fleischmann, the yeast king, who fell off of one of Fisher's polo ponies and died. It is that inevitable Florida anarchy that brought kosher kitchens and Yiddish vaudeville theater, Hungarian food and seltzer trucks, to this pre-planned utopia where civilization started from anti-Semitic scratch.

Bag ladies and women with their stockings rolled around their ankles waddle with their pushcarts. There is a lady down here who yells, "I know who killed Kennedy. I know who killed Kennedy," and if you ask her who, she makes a guttural noise with her tongue. I think she was sent by Ricardo Morales.

The real city has no real industry, now that the tourists go elsewhere. City fathers are asking the same question I am asking myself: who are we? Who are we, in the Florida context, means: why have we lost business? People blame the mobsters gone to Vegas, the jet airplanes that fly overhead full of passengers bound for the Caribbean, the riots in Miami, the waning of Arthur Godfrey, the erosion of the beach, the buildings set too close together blocking out the sun. Miami Beach is a monument to the variance, the city grew up on these permissive riders, with, some say, the bribes attached.

Who are we? discussions begin philosophically and end in pragmatic desperation. When the artist Cristo painted the islands in Biscayne Bay pink and got terrific publicity, one Miami Beach city commissioner proposed that the entire city change its name to Cristo City and paint itself pink. Others seek to bring back gondolas, elephants, singing seals, Fisher's Venetian canals, concrete decorative arches that straddle islands. Florida was never more than an image in the spectator's eye.

I have a preference for failed resorts, and it is Miami Beach's failure I enjoy most of all. Failed resorts are the solace of the pleasure-loving iconoclast. There is a kind of integrity in low occupancy; we sensed it, at first, in Everglades City, one of those unusual Florida places where people were not selling you anything, where you were not the object of their commercial interest. Since so much of the Florida wilderness is uninhabitable, the best substitute for a liberating communion with nature is a communion with distressed real estate.

Around and below the kosher restaurants and the fruit stands is the art deco district, now with full and federal historic designation. Where else in the country can fifty-year-old architecture be deemed historic? It didn't happen with the help of our city fathers—in their search for who we are, the last and the least acceptable suggestion to them is: we are what we were. They resisted the art deco district, perhaps because there is less boodle in preservation than in new construction, perhaps because the glorifying of an actual past defiles the very essence of Florida's appeal, which is an escape from everything real.

New Yorkers and Washingtonians thought the Miami Beach art deco district was worth saving, the Soho crowd, the young Upper West Side aesthetes, artists, writers, cameramen. Barbara Capitman, an energetic woman who came here from Pittsburgh, enlisted the supporters, got the designations, inspired the art deco movement. Friends of mine, who came to Miami Beach only to visit their older relatives, now had a reason to like Miami Beach themselves. On the frontispieces of $150-a-week pullmanettes with hot-plate kitchens are jolly designs, the two- and three-story hotels and apartment buildings are painted up like so many Aztec souvenirs, arranged in a straight line along Ocean Drive for sixteen blocks, and facing the oil-field beach.

Back to the sea, the art deco poster says. The district has brought us back, people too young to have come here in the first place, people who grew up in the 1960s, an era too serious to be adopted as nostalgia, skipping a generation, deciding to remember the Big Bands.

It is art deco weekend in the district. On the porch of the Cardozo Hotel and next door at the Carlyle they are offering wine, beer, and champagne. On the other side of the street is a four-block stretch of cabanas where you can buy art deco lamps, old postcards, ziggurat butter trays, small appliances from the Truman period. Four blocks of art deco treasures, displayed in open air and in full view of the rental units whose elderly inhabitants lived through all this stuff, inhabitants who can't afford to repurchase this refuse of their lives and probably wouldn't buy it even if they could.

Out on the beach is a hot dog stand, its patrons are mostly Latin Americans who don't appreciate art deco. Along the street in front of the Cardozo and the Carlyle hotels are life-sized cardboard reproductions of F. Scott Fitzgerald characters, stood up like targets. Don Goldie and His Jazz Express are playing a forties song, a seventies woman in a fifties dress and with a thirties hat is dancing. Beyond the jazz band are the chickees of Seminole Indians, permanent structures that clash with the hotels. The jazz saxophone clashes with the electric guitar from a country band set up a block south.

Through and around the Fitzgerald mock-ups prance Mexicans in studded black pants, Mexicans with marimbas and fluegelhorns. They are playing "La Adelita" and "La Cucaracha." They end up on the porch of the Carlyle. The Carlyle has recently been purchased by Cavanagh Properties, its old business retirement subdivisions on the Florida west coast. Allies of Leonard Rosen; in Florida, everything reverts to the essence. Cavanagh or its subsidiaries have emerged twice from Chapter 11 bankruptcy, first in Florida land and later in Atlantic City real estate. The porch gossip is that they look out across this stretch of seven art deco hotels they have purchased from the art-deco believers and they ask "Who are we?" and the answer is: casinos.

Inside the Carlyle, at the bar, a man is looking at his watch by the light of his cigarette lighter, a la George Raft.

I am sitting on the Carlyle porch, drinking wine, listening to the simulcast of Mexican fluegelhorns, the jazz saxophone, the electric guitar, peering at the Fitzgerald mock-ups and through the deco tents, out across the oil fields and into the Atlantic beyond, having a great time, liberated by absurdity.

Afterword

Dwight D. Eisenhower, former two-timing president (but never in the Oval Office), once said, "Things are more like they are now than they ever were before." This sums up what's happened in my home state since *Up for Grabs* first appeared in print. The biggest difference between then and now is 5 million more Floridians, and the majority got here by car, boat, or plane, not through the delivery room.

Like mules, retirees don't reproduce, but there's always more where they came from. Deceased retirees (many exported for burial) are replaced by a new batch of living retirees, giving Florida a continuous and expanding supply. Meanwhile, from the south, we get an unending stream of refugees from poverty, warfare, and Castro.

In the old days, Florida filled up from the north end. Now it receives newcomers from both directions, as the Latin influence creeps up and the Peoria influence creeps down. The story of the 1980s was repeated in the 1990s and promises to repeat again in the 2000s—a migratory tsunami. Thus, the average inhabitant continues to identify with Michigan, Cuba, or Peru while enjoying sunshine and low taxes, and lamenting a shortage of prison cells that necessitates favorable plea bargains for convicted felons.

The greatest concentration of Florida natives (the state's least publicized minority) can be found at the upper end of the state and inland from the coasts. Inland Florida still has a lot of green space, or what my Florida-born daughter calls "wasted real estate." Along the coastal perimeter, whenever there's no condo within fifty yards of you, chances are you're standing at the center of a golf course.

No amount of zoning and planning can stop the developers. Overbuilding stops them temporarily, as it did in the condo glut of the late 1980s, but eventually the units are sold, the cranes come back to the coastline, and the dredges are sent out to make new property.

The boom in gated enclaves continues apace. Mechanical arms and security guards keep the various tribes eating, drinking, and puttering with their own kind, except when they bump carts in grocery store aisles or shopping malls or collide on the highways. A rare communal gathering point—the lines at the annual emission control check-up for cars—has just been eliminated.

The Florida described in these pages, I hope, is an accurate reflection of the contemporary scene, where madness and mayhem coexist with carefree boredom and assigned parking spaces. I'm using the rest of this afterword to bring you up to date on a few notable developments, mostly from the capital of madness and mayhem, Miami. In this Q and A format, I've saved time and effort by answering my own Qs.

Do My Parents Still Live in Georgia?

Having escaped from Florida to Georgia in the late 1960s, my parents reversed course in the late 1990s and headed for Miami. This move amazed their friends in the mountains, who thought of Miami as the Beirut of the Western Hemisphere. While my father volunteered at the local New World Symphony, my mother volunteered at a thrift store that donated the proceeds to the fight against AIDS. In the 1960s, she had sold fancy dresses to women at her retail store in St. Petersburg. In the 1990s, she sold those same dresses to men.

What's Up with the Everglades?

I struck up a friendship with Marjory Stoneman Douglas, the cantankerous defender of the Everglades, in the 1980s, when she was in her nineties. She was frail and nearly blind at this point, and her hearing was bad. In her floppy hats and dark glasses she looked like Igor Stravinsky at the Easter parade. In spite of her age and her physical limitations, she could scare the bejesus out of reporters, politicians, bureaucrats, developers, lobbyists, and polluters. People who assumed they could gain her support by giving her awards or naming things after her (she was receiving a tribute a week at one point) often were unpleasantly surprised.

The last time I saw Marjory, we had a dinner date. This was thirteen years into our relationship—she was 103. I'd planned to bring the dinner to her house, but she insisted I make a reservation at Le Festival in Coral Gables, where the waiters spoke French. She said she wanted to brush up on her Romance languages.

Before agreeing to Marjory's plan, I called a mutual acquaintance and asked, "Is there any problem taking a 103-year-old to a restaurant?" "Only one I can think of," she said. "Don't let her drink a Manhattan. Her body can't handle it. A few sips and she's snockered."

I brought fellow writer Jack McClintock along as a backup. The staff met us at the door and spoke French to Marjory, and we were ushered to a table. Marjory ordered a Manhattan.

I'd called in advance to prepare for this moment, and the restaurant was alerted to provide a watered-down version. But as the waiter distributed the drinks, I sensed a problem. "Is that a real Manhattan?" I whispered. The waiter nodded yes, just as Marjory's hands searched for the glass. She couldn't see it, of course, and I managed to pull it away before her fingers had found it.

"Yours isn't here yet," I said matter-of-factly. "Water this down," I told the waiter, *sotto voce*. A few minutes later, he returned with the Shirley Templified version. Marjory sniffed it suspiciously. I figured my ruse had failed. "This Manhattan tastes funny," she announced. "It's too strong!" The waiter hustled to the bar to add a bit more water. For some reason, this version passed Marjory's taste test.

I'm telling you this to show that people went to great lengths not to cross this formidable presence, even at her advanced age. I didn't have the courage to deny her a Manhattan and risk a confrontation, just as the State of Florida itself avoided a confrontation by not inviting her to celebrate the passage of the Everglades Forever Act.

The Everglades Forever Act, formerly known as the Marjory Stoneman Douglas Act, was touted as the salvation of that fragile water system, which for decades has served as a dumping ground for sugar farmers around Lake Okeechobee. In 1994, Governor Lawton Chiles and U.S. Secretary of the Interior Bruce Babbitt walked into the national park and fed the mosquitoes as Chiles signed the paperwork. After hearing the fine print (somebody read her the details), Marjory demanded that her name be removed from the legislation. The state took it a step further and left Marjory off the guest list for the party when the act became law in Tallahassee.

Everglades Forever turned out to be as watered-down as Marjory's Manhattan. Though the act was publicized as tough on polluters in general and sugar companies in particular, the details suggest otherwise. The polluters will continue to pollute until 2006, and their share of the clean-up costs is limited to less than half the estimated total. The public gets stuck with the balance. Environmentalists continue to doubt that the state can be trusted to enforce the act's provisions. The feds have already sued Florida for failure to maintain water quality in the Everglades, and the state has admitted its laxity.

As of this writing, politicians and special interests dither over a $7.8 billion plan to add water to the Everglades, while the state bumbles along with the clean-up. The feds have agreed to pick up half the tab for the new project, but as of now a deadline looms, and interested parties on the Florida side of the deal have failed to reach agreement. If they don't, U.S. Senator Bob Smith (R, New Hampshire) predicts, "We're going to lose the Everglades."

Did Any of the Real Estate Scoundrels I Write About Ever Go to Jail?

Many square miles of empty lots can still be found on Florida's west coast, archaeological mementos to the land scams of prior decades. In 1990, criminal charges were lodged against the General Development Corporation and its honchos. GDC had sold 400,000 home sites in Port Malabar and Port St. Lucie at rigged prices. The company declared bankruptcy, and four principals admitted guilt in a plea bargain. A judge threw out the bargain, and the admittedly felonious foursome was tried and convicted of fraud-related charges in 1992, and sent to the slammer in 1994. Two years later, in a stunning reversal, a Florida appeals court overturned the convictions.

The honchos were liberated, avoiding years of additional jail time, while homeowners, shareholders, and other victims of their salesmanship got back only a fraction of their $5 billion estimated losses. The appellate judges didn't dispute the fact that GDC had put an absurdly high price tag on the real estate, but they ruled that any buyer "of ordinary prudence" could have smelled the rat. "Fornicat emptor," wrote *Miami Herald* columnist Carl Hiaasen. "Let the buyer be screwed."

How Did South Beach Get So Trendy?

When *Up for Grabs* appeared in 1985, Miami was page-one crime news nationwide. Then the gossip columnists moved in, and the press stopped writing about criminals in favor of writing about celebrities such as Don Johnson, Madonna, Sylvester Stallone, Prince, and Mickey Rourke. Once a favorite destination for desperadoes escaping detection, Miami had become a favorite destination for people eager to be seen.

I first became aware of this change when the late Jon Bradshaw, a bourbon-slugging, safari-jacketed journalist in the Hemingway mode, was sent to town by *Vanity Fair*. He spent a week or so interviewing the usual suspects and wrote a long and intriguing update on drugs, spies, scams and hustles, and the latest indictments being handed down—in other words, the typical Miami dispatch from the 1980s. Tina Brown, then editor of *Vanity Fair*, killed Bradshaw's article. She didn't want grist. She wanted glitz.

This was the beginning of the glitz phase that turned Miami Beach's Ocean Drive from low-cost retirement housing into a raucous pleasure strip and the entire area into a celebrity watch: Michael Caine sighted at the Delano Hotel! Steffi Graf sighted on Washington Avenue! Leona Helmsley buys mansion on Star Island! Madonna blows kisses at Miami Heat point guard!

The Miami Beach comeback is as miraculous as Lazarus rising from his tomb wearing a G-string. If you lay down and went to sleep under a palm tree in 1986, you were surrounded by widows wrapped in scarves and speaking Yiddish. A decade later, you woke up to bathing beauties wrapped in camera crews and marinated in coconut oil. On a personal note, it was disconcerting to be twenty years younger than the crowd in 1986 and twenty years older than the crowd in 1996.

It wasn't the architecture, the re-dredged beach, or the Miami moon that brought visitors to the area. It was *Miami Vice.* Conventional wisdom in the Tourist Bureau had worried that this TV showcase of Miami's criminal element would scare the last tourist out of Dade County. Who knew it would be a worldwide hit—so popular that even drug traffickers got involved in the production?

The waterfront house that appeared in several episodes was owned and occupied by a cocaine importer posing as a wealthy fight promoter. Later, the embarrassing truth came out, and for all anybody knew the homeowner was smuggling drugs through the backyard canal while cops hired to guard the set were admiring the actors.

Through multiple seasons of filming, whenever local residents saw a cluster of patrol cars with flashing lights, we asked ourselves, "Is this a crime scene or a *Miami Vice* episode?" This caused continual confusion. Once I joined a crowd gathered around the crime tape outside a popular Miami Beach restaurant, Osteria Del Teatro. Autograph hounds had their pens and pads at the ready, hoping to get Don Johnson's signature. A half-hour went by before we heard that this was a shooting, not a shoot. A disgruntled kitchen hand had peppered the chef.

A friend who stumbled onto a *Miami Vice* crew, filming a fake drug bust, realized she was standing next to a prominent member of the Medellín cocaine cartel, whose picture she'd seen in the paper. He appeared to be enjoying the action as much as she was.

Without *Miami Vice,* the paint might still be peeling on the Art Deco buildings on Ocean Drive. With *Miami Vice* came a lucrative chain reaction: movie stars attracted cameramen and photo labs, cameramen and photo labs attracted modeling agencies, modeling agencies attracted models, models attracted gawkers, and gawkers attracted wanna-be movie stars. The standard definition of a waiter (a person who waits on tables) did not apply at hip Miami Beach restaurants, where customers waited while waiters struck poses, hoping to be discovered by people posing as directors and talent scouts.

One night at the Strand Restaurant, when an hour had passed with no sign of a breadstick, I found a pay phone near the men's room and ordered a Domino's pizza to be delivered to the table. When the pizza arrived at the door, the maitre d' played the role of the bouncer and refused to let it in.

After Elian Was Kicked Out of Miami, Will Janet Reno Be Allowed Back In?

For anybody who suffered an eight-month power outage in a town without a newspaper, Elian Gonzalez lost his mother on a raft trip to Miami and was saved by dolphins, which helped him keep afloat, and by two passing fishermen—one of whom handled the rescue, while the other handled the talk shows. The rescued boy was adopted by Miami relatives and their extended family of lawyers, and played in a tiny front yard surrounded by TV coverage.

Attorney General Janet Reno, who got her job because she'd never hired an illegal alien housekeeper, was determined to return illegal alien Elian to his native police state. She was aided in this effort by yet another lawyer, who had helped save Bill Clinton from Monica Lewinsky. Elian was snatched from a closet and reunited with his father, who was upgraded from raft to 747 and flown to Washington, where he took in all the sights approved by the Cuban Interests

Section. After receiving a similar upgrade, Elian returned to Cuba more or less over the same escape route his raft had taken. He was reintroduced to Fidel worship and food shortages.

Meanwhile, Miamians are waiting to see whether Reno will order herself returned to Miami, where she's no longer persona grata in Little Havana.

Where's the Magic in the Magic City?

Miami claims a fair number of miracles: weeping trees, the Virgin Mary appearing in a mirror at Elian's house and again in a window at a nearby bank, and so on. A less-publicized episode occurred when a well-connected landscape contractor planted a large batch of palms along local roadways. An alert bureaucrat noticed that many palms were shorter than specified in the purchasing order, and some were missing. Accused of ripping off the taxpayers, the contractor explained: the palms had shrunk of their own accord. This didn't explain the other palms that were lost and unaccounted for. Had these shrunk down to nothing?

While the palms were shrinking, a high-rise on Miami Beach grew eleven stories beyond its boundaries. In this eerie episode, the city had approved fourteen stories and the developer had agreed to fourteen stories, yet somehow the structure shot up to twenty-five stories on the final preconstruction okay. A bystander noticed the discrepancy and alerted authorities. How these extra floors materialized, the city couldn't say. The developer, Thomas Kramer, was mystified as well, but as you'll soon see, Kramer had other things on his mind, mostly skirt-chasing.

In addition to the shrinking palms and burgeoning buildings, defendants in Miami's court system often vanish overnight. Among the crowd of disappearances, several local celebrities stand out.

Local power broker Miguel Recarey disappeared to avoid incarceration in the biggest Medicare swindle in U.S. history. Federal authorities knew of Recarey's whereabouts in Caracas, Venezuela, but apparently made no attempt to have him extradited.

County commissioner Joey Gersten disappeared after his Mercedes vanished from the parking lot of a motel that charged by the hour. Two female witnesses, who also charged by the hour, insisted the commissioner's car was stolen while the threesome shared a bed and a crack pipe. On his release from jail on a contempt-of-court charge for refusing to provide details, Gersten went AWOL and later surfaced in Australia.

In another disappearance involving a vehicle, the supervisor of a cemetery work crew reported his car missing. Later it was found eight feet under in a cemetery plot. The supervisor admitted he had buried it for the insurance money. Obviously, he lacked good legal advice. Any well-informed Miami lawyer would have claimed the car dug its own grave.

Is Miami Still Number One in Drug Smuggling?

Lee Stapleton, chief of narcotics at the U.S. Attorney's Office in Miami, confided the following to the *Miami Herald* in mid-1996: "Business is booming. Cocaine, heroin, and marijuana are dropping out of the sky, being unloaded at sea, and being moved up and down our rivers and highways. If anything has changed, it's that heroin smuggling has increased drastically over the past few years."

Today, Miami-area DEA squads seize as much cocaine as they nabbed from the cocaine cowboys in the 1980s, but for several reasons nobody cares: (1) *Miami Vice* is a dim memory; (2) the drug business now runs less along the lines of Scarface and more along the lines of AT&T; (3) cocaine was downgraded from glamour toot to ghetto fodder; and (4) everybody realizes that stopping drugs is a lost cause.

In fact, the DEA's Brent Eaton notes the going price for a kilo of coke has dropped from $30,000 to $10,000. The cost of a high continues to drop, while the cost of living rises, a textbook case of what happens when supply outruns demand. South Florida competes with Mexico as the country's busiest import center, but Miami is number one in money laundering, and home to the launderers.

Has the Anti-Castro Faction Mellowed?

A few roads were blocked and a couple of pro-Reno protesters were hustled into police cars to protect them from an angry crowd, but otherwise the Elian protests were peaceable. This suggests that the hard-line exile faction is losing its heavy touch. A generation ago bombings and shootings were common forms of political protest, but as time passed bombs were left in places where nobody was likely to be blown up. In 1988, Miami professor Maria Christina Herrera hosted a conference on Cuban relations (local translation: coddling the enemy). Critics sent a message via the bomb found in her garage. A few years earlier, it might have been tossed through her living room window.

Similarly, when Miami's Cuban Museum of Art and Culture made the political mistake of auctioning off artwork by artists from Cuba, the obligatory bomb was discovered in an abandoned car in the museum parking lot. A local female attorney committed a political gaffe by kissing Castro on the cheek in a Havana receiving line. After the footage was broadcast repeatedly on Miami television, she was threatened and vilified but suffered no bodily harm, unlike the radio commentator who lost his legs for promoting dialogue with Castro in the 1970s.

Older Cubans have lost interest in relocating to their

homeland. This became apparent after the fall of communism in Russia and Central Europe. Thinking the Castro regime would be the next domino to fall, thousands of Miami exiles prepared to swarm Cuba, not as residents but as investors. Cargo ships were loaded with windows and building materials at Miami's docks. Burger King got so many inquiries about Havana franchises that the company started a waiting list. In post-Castro Cuba, Miami Cubans will play the role the gringos played in the 1950s. They'll enjoy the beaches and the nightclubs and own many of the businesses, but they'll reside in the U.S.A.

And in spite of sensational news that suggests the opposite, younger Cuban-Americans are far more American than Cuban. To their grandparents' consternation, they care more about the Miami Heat making the playoffs than about the U.S. embargo against Castro.

Doesn't Anybody Check These Things?

Nobody checked the background of the smuggler who rented the house to *Miami Vice.* Nobody checked the background of numerous felons who received keys to various local municipalities, including Chris Paciello, a wildly popular nightclub owner honored by the City of Miami Beach only months before his arrest for a brutal home invasion robbery back in New York. Paciello a thug—what a surprise! In Miami it's considered rude to pry into the personal histories of any splashy *arriviste*, especially after the newcomer has thrown money at the ballet, the symphony, and key charities and gotten favorable reviews in the local press.

Thirty-four-year-old German jet-setter Thomas Kramer arrived on the scene in 1991 with a wad of cash and a new wife, leaving behind a string of flashy escorts and a longer string of angry investors who got leiderhosed in Kramer's bankrupt East German real estate flop. Within months this unemployed gadabout plunked down $40 million to buy several houses and forty-five acres of South Beach real estate. He distributed his spare cash to prominent charities and got the typical hero's welcome. Quickly, he was put on the boards of American Airlines, the prestigious Ocean Reef Club, and the Knight Foundation, the charitable arm of the *Miami Herald*. He presented himself as a "family man."

In addition to the spare cash, Kramer did his best to provide the local press with fresh copy by punching a restaurant owner who asked him to douse his cigar, and by nonconsensual groping and fondling of numerous women who filed complaints and lawsuits (and in one case had Kramer arrested for rape). Kramer, in other words, was a one-man NBA, NFL, and MLB. He further endeared himself by telling people lined up at his nightclub (at this point, he was on his way to owning everything) that they were "too ugly to get in." For good measure, he reportedly tossed a glass of wine in a panhandler's face and just as reportedly called designer Gianni Versace a "fag," in the Marge Schott tradition. For legal reasons, I'm obliged to add he denied everything, and his aforementioned accuser dropped the rape charge.

Upholding the long-standing good neighbor policy toward traveling scoundrels—as I'm writing this, I'm thinking of a new Miami-area tourist campaign, "Get away from it all while getting away with it all"—Miami Beach city fathers and mothers approved a momentous land swap that gave Kramer the prized southern tip of the city. Kramer had said he planned a tasteful, well-designed complex of low-rises but, once in possession of the land, quickly changed his mind and pushed for a skyscraping eyesore that dwarfs the entire region. The eyesore required numerous variances and waivers on planning and zoning rules, which Kramer was promptly awarded. City commissioners, including three "preservationists," let him build the thing.

For his own lodging, Kramer envisioned a 54,000-square-foot "mosque-style" mansion with five domes and a special fog machine to blow cool air across the lawn. The mosque exceeded the local height restrictions, so he got a variance for that, too, although it might have grown taller on its own. Exercising its familiar "don't ask, don't tell" policy, the establishment press was slow to do a background check. The real story finally broke in the German press, answering the big question: "Where did this rapacious Romeo get all that money?" The source, apparently, was Kramer's ex-wife's stepfather, a German entrepreneur who'd made a fortune in the printing business—not books, but banknotes and currencies. The money printer, who later pleaded guilty to German tax fraud, had shipped Kramer $145 million to invest in real estate. Once apprised of Kramer's Miami Beach spending spree, the stepfather tried to recapture the balance. Whether he succeeded is unclear.

Lately, Kramer has kept an uncharacteristically low profile. He sold the lot where the mosque was supposed to go. The buyer was Leona Helmsley, Queen of Mean, who came here to recuperate from a prison term for *her* tax evasion.

Will Miami Ever Grow Up?

There's a local jubilee in larceny. We've had corruption scandals in the parks department, building codes, the airport, the cruise ship port, landscaping, paving, and a long string of indicted and/or convicted mayors. The Miami finance director, nabbed in a bribe attempt, agreed to trap his superiors in additional bribery attempts. He wore a hidden wire and landed the city manager, a former city manager, a bond broker, and a city commissioner. The bond broker was also wired and landed another county commissioner and a commissioner's aide.

Scandals pop up so regularly that any reader of the *Miami Herald* is soon subjected to post-traumatic sleaze syndrome, which results in numbness, loss of political appetite, and disinterest in voting. We've had a county manager wearing stolen suits. We've had a city manager with a phony diploma on his wall. We've had dead people casting votes. We've had a female mayor arrested for plotting to kill her husband. We've had a male mayor indicted twice for fraud and reelected both times. We've had the "River Cops" privatizing the cocaine trade by busting traffickers and reselling the inventory (investigators estimated 10 percent of the police force may have been involved). We've had "Operation Court Broom," where four judges who took cash for favors and five lawyers were convicted. With typical Miami chutzpah, the judges stuffed wads of bills in envelopes and left them in dresser drawers in their houses, where police had no trouble finding them.

Miami leads the nation in Medicare fraud, and it's right up there in auto fraud. We've had sixty-three doctors and medical personnel arrested in "Operation Big Broom" for filing phony Medicare claims. We've got dentists practicing without a license in spare bedrooms in their homes. We've got phony doctors doing plastic surgery with unsterilized instruments. It tells you something that O. J. Simpson feels comfortable in South Florida.

As an aforementioned city manager prepared to trade pinstripes for broader stripes, his temporary replacement discovered that $27 million in taxpayers' money had vanished from the city till. Auditors combed the financial wreckage, and this figure soon became $37 million, then $60 million, then $67 million—roughly a quarter of the City of Miami's annual budget. This was the magic of the disappearing assets. Soon the state threatened to take over the city's finances, the way it might for a befuddled geriatric.

To ensure that taxpayers got fuller benefits from the taxes that survived the pilfering, the replacement manager ordered employees to turn in their city cars, cellular phones, and gas credit cards, all of which were regularly used for unofficial business. Girlfriends, boyfriends, and relatives of city officials "not hired on merit" were ordered to clean their desks of comic books, crossword puzzles, emery boards, and romance novels, and resign their patronage.

"People forget Miami is a young city," political scientist Dario Moreno was quoted as saying after a busy scandal season. "Like any rebellious adolescent," echoed journalist David Adams, "Miami likes to learn its lessons the hard way." This was the "Miami needs time to grow up" excuse first heard at the turn of the century, and repeated ever since.

As described in these pages, the same "immature" Miami rolled out the red carpet for Al Capone in the 1920s, became a playground for retired mobsters in the 1940s, was the target of a Senate crime committee in the 1950s, allowed bookies to operate openly in the lobbies of beachfront hotels in the 1960s, produced the Watergate burglars in the 1970s, embraced the drug trade in the 1980s, and hosted the corruption epidemic of the 1990s.

If crime is a sign of immaturity, then judging by its rap sheet Miami is the true fountain of youth. Corruption trickles up and trickles down through every public institution, and plenty that are private. One courtroom leads to another courtroom and often several courtrooms. In the early 1990s, journalist David Adams punched the words *corruption* and *Miami City Hall* into his computer database. This search produced 3,033 entries back to 1984.

Mark Schnapp, former prosecutor in the U.S. Attorney's Office who now works the defense side, remembers the day when the staying power of Miami's roguery was revealed. He stood at a busy street corner during an election campaign, looking at the various placards and posters taped to trees or lampposts or held aloft by volunteers. "That's when I realized," he said, "that I'd indicted every one of these candidates for one crime or another. I wish I'd taken a snapshot."

Is Miami for Real?

Not always. Miami's a pretender's paradise. Home invaders pretend to be cops; cops pretend to be drug dealers; men pretend to be women; the leading savings-and-loan villain, now incarcerated, pretended to graduate from Harvard (his actual alma mater, Columbia, wasn't good enough?); a county manager pretended he had a master's degree from Utah, was found out, and still got hired for the job. "Even though . . . he had spoken of a degree," a commissioner said, "he was cleared of lying because he had never claimed in writing to have the degree."

The same man with the faux master's was caught wearing hot suits—not wool but stolen. It wasn't just him. A number of public servants bought their suits from a one-room "store" conveniently located near City Hall, where merchandise was stuffed in boxes, piled on the floor, or hung on makeshift racks. It looked suspicious, but the price was right so customers pretended the store was legit.

A female financial planner, who beat out Janet Reno as Dade County's outstanding businesswoman of the year, pretended to be a cancer survivor and put her clients into pretend investments. A $150-a-week insurance salesman landed a $20 million construction contract with the county. In his promotional brochure, he claimed two Purple Hearts, an MBA degree from the University of Southern California, seven seasons with the Dallas Cowboys, and a black belt in karate. All this, on top of his careers as a race car driver, professional boxer, certified hospital operating technician, Navy Seals demolition expert, and the number-one-rated disc jockey in Detroit.

Nobody balked until a young *Miami Herald* reporter, Bettina Charles, decided to check his story with the Dallas Cowboys, who had no record of the alleged player. A year after Charles's exposé appeared, the great pretender became a star—a star witness in a bribery case (what else?) against the county purchasing chief.

Is This Utopia or What?

In 1996, Walt Disney World celebrated its twenty-fifth anniversary in Orlando. The $5 million it paid for 27,000 acres in 1971 wouldn't buy five acres of prime Disney real estate today. The scorecard on Disney World looked like this: 46 square miles, 3 theme parks, 3 water parks, 2 theater and nightclub centers, 27 hotels and campgrounds with 22,400 hotel rooms, 246 eateries, 6 golf courses, a bayside marketplace with a man-made bay, and 80 swimming pools and/or lakes. Right now 33 million people pass through the turnstiles annually, and Disney watchers predicted the place will grow into 5 theme parks and 70,000 hotel rooms and attract an annual 100 million visitors—more than half the adult population of the U.S.A.

So there's more Disney in Orlando, more Orlando in general, and the line between Disney and non-Disney is progressively blurred. Disney characters can be seen roaming the airport and are loaned out to conventions and other public functions. People can live in the Disney town of Celebration, fifteen minutes south of Cinderella's Castle.

I drove to Orlando to witness Celebration's grand opening in the early 1990s. This was Disney's first foray into the real world, and thousands gathered in the former cow pasture to enter a drawing to become pioneer inhabitants. They were anxious to inhabit a fairy-tale suburb that only Disney "imagineering" could create.

Walt Disney himself had the original idea for a dream town where inhabitants were whooshed from skyscraper to skyscraper on a speedy monorail. In Disney's version, no retirees were allowed and nobody could own property. He expected to fill the skyscrapers with renters. I figure that by replacing the renters as they matured, he could keep the place eternally young. Disney died in 1966 before the plans were drawn up.

From on-site interviews at Celebration, I found out what potential buyers hoped to find in a dream town in the 1990s: decent schools, clean streets, nice parks, low crime. In other words, a regular town from the 1950s, 1960s, or even the 1970s. What was normal then was now considered so fantastic, only Disney could provide it.

Ten years later, Celebration turns out to be less fantastic than its pioneers expected. They've had parents bitching about the school, homeowners bitching about shoddy contractors, nonresidents bitching about too little rainbow in the ethnic makeup, and a dangerous curve that has dunked several cars into a lake and produced at least four drowning fatalities, several near fatalities, and extra work for divers.

If the Place Is So Corrupt, So Gaudy, So Shameless, So Careless, So Scurrilous, So Felonious, and So Silly, Why Do You Still Live in Miami Beach?

It's got sunshine, close proximity to the airport, and Cuban coffee, and if you take the long-term view that in 1,000 years nobody will care about the problems, Miami is the greatest show on earth.